LAW, CRIME AND LAW ENFORCEMENT

FEDERAL MANDATORY MINIMUM SENTENCING:

SEXUAL OFFENSES AND AGGRAVATED IDENTITY THEFT

LAW, CRIME AND LAW ENFORCEMENT

Additional books in this series can be found on Nova's website under the Series tab.

Additional E-books in this series can be found on Nova's website under the E-book tab.

LAWS AND LEGISLATION

Additional books in this series can be found on Nova's website under the Series tab.

Additional E-books in this series can be found on Nova's website under the E-book tab.

LAW, CRIME AND LAW ENFORCEMENT

FEDERAL MANDATORY MINIMUM SENTENCING:

SEXUAL OFFENSES AND AGGRAVATED IDENTITY THEFT

MICHAEL J. DAVIS
AND
ABIGAIL M. WHITE
EDITORS

Nova Science Publishers, Inc.
New York

For permission to use material from this book please contact us:
Telephone 631-231-7269; Fax 631-231-8175
Web Site: http://www.novapublishers.com

Additional color graphics may be available in the e-book version of this book.

Library of Congress Cataloging-in-Publication Data

ISBN: 978-1-62081-988-3

Published by Nova Science Publishers, Inc. †New York

CONTENTS

PREFACE

Sex offenses are usually hate crimes. Federal law, however, outlaws sex offenses when they occur on federal lands or in federal prisons, when they involve interstate or foreign travel, or when they involve child pornography whose production or distribution is associated in some way with interstate or foreign commerce. Mandatory minimum terms of imprisonment attend conviction for any of several of these federal sex crimes. Aggravated identity theft is punishable by a mandatory minimum sentence of imprisonment for two years or by imprisonment for five years if it relates to a terrorism offense. The two-year offense occurs when an individual knowingly possesses, uses, or transfers the means of identification of another person, without lawful authority to do so, during and in relation to one of more than 60 predicate federal felony offenses. This book provides an overview of federal mandatory minimum sentencing law with regard to sexual offenses and aggravated identity theft, specifically.

Chapter 1 - Sex offenses are usually state crimes. Federal law, however, outlaws sex offenses when they occur on federal lands or in federal prisons, when they involve interstate or foreign travel, or when they involve child pornography whose production or distribution is associated in some way with interstate or foreign commerce. Mandatory minimum terms of imprisonment attend conviction for any of several of these federal sex crimes.

The most severe mandatory minimum sentences have been reserved for aggravated sexual assaults committed in federal enclaves or federal prisons, for sex offenses resulting in death, and for sex crimes committed against children by repeat offenders.

Two-thirds of the federal trial judges responding to a U.S. Sentencing Commission survey questioned the severity of the mandatory minimum penalties required for receipt of child pornography (5 years; 15 years for repeat offenders). The Commission's report suggested that the perception may lead to inconsistent sentencing in child pornography cases. It explained that more study would be required before it could make any specific recommendations concerning mandatory minimum sentencing in sex offenses.

The constitutional authority to enact federal sex offense punishable by mandatory minimum terms of imprisonment is not unlimited. The ex post facto and double jeopardy clauses; the Fifth Amendment's equal protection component; the Eighth Amendment's cruel and unusual punishment clause; the separation of powers and the reservation of powers principles—all establish boundaries that must be honored. Nevertheless, few defendants have successfully challenged the constitutionality of a mandatory minimum term of imprisonment imposed following their conviction for a federal sex offense.

Chapter 2 - Aggravated identity theft is punishable by a mandatory minimum sentence of imprisonment for two years or by imprisonment for five years if it relates to a terrorism offense. At least thus far, the government has rarely prosecuted the five-year terrorism form of the offense. The two-year offense occurs when an individual knowingly possesses, uses, or transfers the means of identification of another person, without lawful authority to do so, during and in relation to one of more than 60 predicate federal felony offenses (18 U.S.C. 1028A). Section 1028A has the effect of establishing a mandatory minimum sentence for those predicate felony offenses, when they involve identity theft.

A sentencing court has the discretion not to "stack" or pancake multiple aggravated identity theft counts and, as with other mandatory minimums, may impose a sentence of less than the mandatory minimum at the request of the prosecution based on the defendant's substantial assistance.

More than half of the judges responding to a United States Sentence Commission survey felt the two-year mandatory minimum penalty was generally appropriate. The commission's report on mandatory minimum sentencing statutes is mildly complimentary of the provision.

In: Federal Mandatory Minimum Sentencing ISBN 978-1-62081-988-3
Editors: M. J. Davis and A. M. White

Chapter 1

MANDATORY MINIMUM SENTENCING FOR FEDERAL SEX OFFENSES: AN OVERVIEW*

Charles Doyle

SUMMARY

Sex offenses are usually state crimes. Federal law, however, outlaws sex offenses when they occur on federal lands or in federal prisons, when they involve interstate or foreign travel, or when they involve child pornography whose production or distribution is associated in some way with interstate or foreign commerce. Mandatory minimum terms of imprisonment attend conviction for any of several of these federal sex crimes.

The most severe mandatory minimum sentences have been reserved for aggravated sexual assaults committed in federal enclaves or federal prisons, for sex offenses resulting in death, and for sex crimes committed against children by repeat offenders.

Two-thirds of the federal trial judges responding to a U.S. Sentencing Commission survey questioned the severity of the mandatory minimum penalties required for receipt of child pornography (5 years; 15 years for repeat offenders). The Commission's report suggested that the perception may lead to inconsistent sentencing in child pornography cases. It explained that more

* This is an edited, reformatted and augmented version of the Congressional Research Service Publication, CRS Report for Congress R42386, dated March 2, 2012.

study would be required before it could make any specific recommendations concerning mandatory minimum sentencing in sex offenses.

The constitutional authority to enact federal sex offense punishable by mandatory minimum terms of imprisonment is not unlimited. The ex post facto and double jeopardy clauses; the Fifth Amendment's equal protection component; the Eighth Amendment's cruel and unusual punishment clause; the separation of powers and the reservation of powers principles—all establish boundaries that must be honored. Nevertheless, few defendants have successfully challenged the constitutionality of a mandatory minimum term of imprisonment imposed following their conviction for a federal sex offense.

INTRODUCTION

A mandatory minimum sentencing statute is a law that requires a judge to impose a statutorily prescribed sentence. It is most commonly understood to mean a statute that requires imposition of a specific minimum term of imprisonment. The statutes that outlaw most federal crimes do not call for a mandatory minimum sentence. Several statutes that outlaw federal sex offenses insist upon a minimum term of imprisonment. This is a brief overview of those provisions.[1]

BACKGROUND

Mandatory minimum sentences have been with us since the dawn of the Republic. The First Congress made mandatory capital offenses of treason, murder in a federal enclave, piracy, forgery, and counterfeiting.[2] A few years later, the Sedition and Logan Acts arrived with six-month mandatory minimum terms of imprisonment.[3] Congress made rape committed within the maritime jurisdiction of the United States a mandatory capital offense in 1825.[4] So the punishment remained until the 1948 recodification of federal criminal law, when rape became punishable by death or imprisonment for any term of years or for life.[5]

Congress increased the number of federal sex offenses and their attendant mandatory minimum sentences beginning in 1978 with the enactment of the first federal child pornography statutes: 18 U.S.C. 2251, 2252.[6] It filled out the complement of federal sex offenses with mandatory minimum sentences of imprisonment at fairly regular intervals thereafter.[7]

In United States Sentencing Commission survey which addressed mandatory minimum sentences in child pornography cases but not other sex offense cases, a majority of the judges responding to a United States Sentencing Commission survey thought that the mandatory minimum sentences for production and distribution of child pornography and other child exploitation offenses were generally appropriate. Well over two-thirds, however, considered those for receipt of child pornography too high.[8]

The Commission's report on mandatory minimum sentencing statutes noted that its "review of available sentencing data [relating to sex offenses] indicates that further study of these penalties is needed before it can offer specific recommendations in this area."[9] It concluded preliminarily, however, that "the mandatory minimum penalties for certain non-contact child pornography offenses may be excessively severe and as a result are being applied inconsistently."[10]

What Is a Mandatory Minimum?

There may be reasonable disagreement over what constitutes a mandatory minimum sentencing statute. Even when limited to statutes that require a minimum term of imprisonment, questions may arise with respect to: (1) statutes like 18 U.S.C. 2241(c) (sexual abuse of a child) that requires offenders to be imprisoned for not less than 30 years or for life; (2) statutes like 18 U.S.C. 2242 (sexual abuse of an incapacitated victim) that requires offenders to be fined and imprisoned for any term of years or for life; and (3) statutes like 18 U.S.C. 2241(a)(aggravated sexual abuse) that requires offenders to be fined, imprisoned for any term of years or life, or both.

Subsection 2241(c) certainly appears to require a mandatory minimum sentence ("imprisoned not less than 30 years").[11] Section 2242 also appears to require a mandatory minimum sentence, absent the dubious conclusion that the phrase, "imprisonment for any term of years" authorizes a court to impose a sentence of imprisonment for some particular number of years with the permissible choices ranging from zero to infinity.[12]

The mandatory minimum status of subsection 2241(a)("fine [or] imprisonment for any term of years") seems more debatable. The subsection can hardly be said to require a mandatory minimum sentence of imprisonment, if a court is free to impose a fine instead. Moreover, in another context, the courts have concluded that in the face of such language a court is free to impose a fine instead of a term of imprisonment.[13] Nevertheless, it is treated as requiring a mandatory minimum sentence here, because as a practical matter a court is virtually required to impose a sentence of imprisonment following conviction for a crime as serious as a violation of subsection 2241(a).[14]

CONSTITUTIONAL CONSIDERATIONS

Defendants sentenced to mandatory minimum terms of imprisonment have challenged them on a number of constitutional grounds ranging from Congress's legislative authority, to cruel and unusual punishment, through ex post facto and double jeopardy, to equal protection and due process. Each constitutional provision defines the outer boundaries that a federal criminal statute must be crafted to honor. Most statutes and the penalties they impose have survived scrutiny.

Legislative Authority

The federal government is a creature of the Constitution.[15] It enjoys only such powers as can be traced to the Constitution. All other powers are reserved to the states or to the people.[16] The Constitution grants Congress authority to enact legislation "necessary and proper" to the execution of those powers which it vests in Congress or in any officer or department of the federal government.[17] Among the powers which the Constitution bestows upon Congress are the powers to define and punish felonies committed upon the high seas, to exercise exclusive legislative authority over certain federal territories and facilities, to make rules governing the armed forces, and to regulate interstate and foreign commerce, and to enact legislation necessary and proper for the execution of those and other constitutionally granted powers.[18]

Many of the existing federal sex offenses with mandatory minimum sentencing requirements were enacted pursuant to Congress's legislative authority over crimes occurring on the high seas or within federal enclaves,[19] or to its power to regulate commerce.[20]

The Supreme Court has explained that under the commerce clause: "Congress may regulate the use of the channels of interstate commerce.

Second, Congress is empowered to regulate and protect the instrumentalities of interstate commerce, or persons or things in interstate commerce, even though the threat may come only from intrastate activities. Finally, Congress' commerce authority includes the power to regulate those activities having a substantial relation to interstate commerce."[21] When a statute falls for want of legislative authority, the penalties it would impose fall with it. This has yet to occur in the area of mandatory minimum sentences.

Cruel and Unusual Punishment

The Eighth Amendment bars mandatory capital punishment statutes.[22] And although the case law is somewhat uncertain, it seems the Amendment condemns any punishment that is "grossly disproportionate" to the misconduct for which it is imposed.[23] A sentence imposed under a mandatory minimum federal sex offense statute might be "grossly disproportionate" to the offense under extreme circumstances, but the sentences in most cases are not.[24]

Separation of Powers

While "it remains a basic principle of our constitutional scheme that one branch of the Government may not intrude upon the central prerogatives of another,"[25] the Supreme Court has observed that "Congress has the power to define criminal punishments without giving the courts any sentencing discretion."[26] Thus, the lower federal courts have regularly upheld mandatory minimum statutes when challenged on separation of powers grounds,[27] and the Supreme Court found no separation of powers infirmity in the federal sentencing guideline system, a system which might have been thought to produce its own form of mandatory minimums.[28]

Equal Protection

The Fifth Amendment due process clause embodies an equal protection component that cabins federal action in the manner that the Fourteenth Amendment equal protection clause cabins state action.[29] Equal protection precludes punishing a defendant more severely than others similarly situated, when the distinction is based on some constitutionally suspect classification such as race or alternatively when the distinction has no rational basis.[30] However, a defendant convicted of a federal sex crime has no equal protection claim, simply because he might have been less severely punished under state law or because he might have been charged with a less serious federal offense.[31]

Equal protection also prohibits punishment, under a facially neutral statute, that is intended to have an adverse impact on a constitutionally protected class.[32] Yet, the presence of a rational basis for a classification will belie an intent to adversely impact. Thus, Native Americans, who may be more likely to come within the reach of federal criminal laws applicable on federal lands, have no equal protection claim as long as Congress had a rational basis for enacting such laws.[33]

Recidivism, Ex Post Facto and Double Jeopardy

Defendants whose prior convictions trigger a mandatory minimum sentencing requirement have occasionally objected on double jeopardy or ex post facto grounds. Double jeopardy bans trying or punishing a defendant twice for the same offense.[34] Ex post facto bars retroactive criminal statutes.[35] More precisely, the double jeopardy clause "protects against successive prosecutions for the same offense after acquittal or conviction and against multiple criminal punishments for the same offense."[36] The ex post facto clauses, on the other hand, preclude laws that "retroactively alter the definition of crimes or [retroactively] increase the punishment for criminal acts."[37]

As the Supreme Court explained when it rejected the double jeopardy challenge to the California "three strikes" statute:

> Historically, we have found double jeopardy protections inapplicable to sentencing proceedings, because the determinations at issue do not place a defendant in jeopardy for an "offense," see *e.g., Nichols v. United States*, 511 U.S. 738, 747 (1994)(noting that repeat-offender laws "penaliz[e] only the last offense committed by the defendant"). Nor have sentence enhancements been construed as additional punishment for the previous offense; rather, they act to increase a sentence "because of the manner in which [the defendant] committed the crime of conviction." An enhanced sentence imposed on a persistent offender thus "is not to be viewed as either a new jeopardy or additional penalty for the earlier crimes" but as "a stiffened penalty for the latest crime which is considered to be an aggravated offense

because a repetitive one." *Monge v. California*, 524 U.S. at 728 (some citations omitted).[38]

Courts confronted with ex post facto challenges to recidivist statutes have similarly focused upon the "latest crime" and not upon the first.[39]

FEDERAL ENCLAVES AND PRISONS

Most of the mandatory minimum penalties for federal sex offenses appear in one of three chapters of title 18 of the United States Code. Chapter 109A outlaws rape and other forms of sexual abuse and sexual contact when committed in federal enclaves or federal prisons. Chapter 110 outlaws child pornography. Chapter 117 outlaws sexual activities that have travel or commercial attributes.

Chapter 109A reaches a relatively wide range of sexual misconduct under relatively narrow jurisdiction circumstances. It applies in the special maritime and territorial jurisdiction of the United States. It applies as well in federal prisons and other institutions where individuals are held in federal custody by contract or agreement with federal authorities, regardless of whether they are located within the territorial jurisdiction of the United States.[40]

Within the United States, the "territorial jurisdiction of the United States" refers to those areas over which Congress enjoys state-like legislative jurisdiction.[41] It includes some, or parts of some, military installations, Indian reservations, national parks, and national forests.[42] Outside of the United States, it includes overseas federal facilities and residences with respect to offenses committed by or against U.S. nationals.[43] Felonies proscribed when committed within the territorial jurisdiction of the United States are also proscribed when committed outside the United States by members of the Armed Forces, or employees of the Armed Forces, or those accompanying the Armed Forces.[44]

The "maritime jurisdiction of the United States" includes vessels of U.S. registry, vessels owned by Americans, and vessels scheduled to arrive in, or depart from, the United States with respect to crimes committed by or against a U.S. national.[45]

Prosecution of the mandatory minimum offenses of chapter 109A and each of the other mandatory minimum federal sex offenses may begin at anytime.[46] There is no applicable statute of limitations, although in rare instances due process may preclude prosecution of a stale complaint.[47]

Chapter 109A Offenses

Chapter 109A violations trigger mandatory minimum sentencing provisions when:

- the offender commits or attempts to commit a sexual act by force or threat or by rendering the victim unconscious or intoxicated (aggravated sexual abuse);[48]
- a sexual act is committed against a minor under the age of 12, or under the age of 16, if is there is disparity of 4 years or more between the age of the victim and the age of the offender (aggravated sexual abuse of a child);[49]
- the offender commits or attempts to commit a sexual act by threat or when the victim is incapacitated (sexual abuse);[50]
- had the sexual contact been a sexual act, it would have been punishable as sexual abuse or aggravated sexual abuse (abusive sexual contact);[51] or
- the offense is a federal sex offense, including an offense subject to a mandatory minimum sentence, committed against a minor by an offender with a prior state or federal conviction for a sex offense committed against a minor (repeated sexual offense).[52]

Definitions

Chapter 109A offenses each involve some form of "sexual act" or "sexual contact." The term "sexual act" includes oral sexual activity as well as sexual penetration by sex organ, foreign object, or digitally.[53] It also covers touching the genitalia of a child under the age of 16 for purposes of humiliation or sexual gratification.[54] The term "sexual contact" includes touching any of the sexually sensitive areas of the body of another for purposes of humiliation or sexual gratification.[55]

Aggravated Sexual Abuse

Section 2241 of chapter 109A proscribes two types of aggravated sexual abuse, each punishable by a mandatory minimum term of imprisonment. First, under the prison and territorial conditions noted above, subsections 2241(a) and (b) outlaw causing, or attempting to cause, another person to engage in a sexual act, when it is accomplished by force, threat, rendering the victim unconscious, or by substantially incapacitating the victim using drugs or intoxicants.[56] Such misconduct is punishable by fine, or by imprisonment for any term of years or for life, or by both a fine and imprisonment, regardless of the age of the victim.[57]

Second, under prison and territorial conditions or when the offender crosses a state border with intent to commit the offense, subsection 2241(c) criminalizes engaging or attempting to engage in a sexual act with a child under 12 years of age (or under 16 years of age, if the offender is 4 years or more the victim's senior).[58] The offense is punishable by imprisonment for not less than 30 years or for life.[59] The mandatory minimum sentencing requirement cannot be overcome by the general sentencing instruction in 18 U.S.C. 3553(a) that a sentence imposed should be no greater than necessary to serve the sentencing purposes identified in that section.[60] The offense is punishable by life imprisonment, if the offender has a prior comparable federal or state conviction.[61]

A defendant may be guilty of an attempted violation of subsection 2241(a), (b), or (c), when he intends to commit the offense and takes a substantial step towards its completion.[62] The prosecution under subsection 2241(c) need not show that the defendant knew that the victim was under 12 years of age,[63] and the greater protection afforded victims under the age of 12 offends neither the equal protection nor due process clauses of the Constitution.[64] The courts have held that a 30-year mandatory minimum sentence for violation of subsection 2241(c) is not so disproportionate as to constitute unconstitutional cruel and unusual punishment,[65] nor does its imposition upon Native Americans violate the equal protection clause.[66] Although abusive sexual contact is a lesser included offense of aggravated sexual abuse, both may be prosecuted without offending the double jeopardy clause, when they involve distinct criminal acts, even if occurring in the same criminal episode.[67]

Sexual Abuse

Section 2242 makes sexual abuse a federal crime when comparable jurisdiction conditions exist, that is, when it is committed within the special maritime and territorial jurisdiction of the United States or equivalent overseas locations or in a federal prison or other federal custodial institution.[68] Sexual abuse is punishable by a fine and a mandatory minimum term of imprisonment for any term of years or for life, regardless of the age of the victim.[69] The offense may be committed by using or attempting to use threats to cause another to engage in a sexual act or by engaging or attempting to engage in a sexual act with an incapacitated victim.[70] A victim who is asleep or incapacitated by intoxication is considered incapacitated for purposes of sexual abuse.[71] A victim with reduced mental capacity may also be considered more susceptible to threats.[72]

Abusive Sexual Contact

Section 2244 proscribes abusive sexual contact, that is, engaging in sexual contact (touching) under circumstances (threats, force, etc.) that would constitute abuse under section 2241 or 2242 had the contact been a sexual act (penetration).[73] Abusive sexual contact is punishable by a fine and a mandatory term of imprisonment for any term of years or for life when engaging in a sexual act under similar circumstances would have violated subsection 2241(c)(victim under 12 or under 16 if the offender is more than 4 years the victim's senior).[74] Abusive sexual contact is not otherwise punishable by a mandatory minimum term of imprisonment.[75]

Repeated Sex Offenses against Children

A defendant, guilty of a "federal sex offense" against a child and previously convicted of a federal or state felonious sex offense committed against a child, must be sentenced to life imprisonment under 18 U.S.C. 3559(e).[76] A child for purposes of subsection 3559(e) is a minor under the age of 17.[77] The federal predicate offenses for purposes of the subsection include both violations of chapter 109A and similar federal and state offenses, that is, violations of "section 1591 (relating to sex trafficking of children), 2241 (relating to aggravated sexual abuse), 2242 (relating to sexual abuse), 2244(a)(1) (relating to abusive sexual contact), 2245 (relating to sexual abuse resulting in death), 2251 (relating to sexual exploitation of children), 2251A (relating to selling or buying of children), 2422(b) (relating to coercion and enticement of a minor into prostitution), 2423(a) (relating to transportation of minors);" or any state equivalent felony.[78]

The defendant must also have been convicted and sentenced prior to the commission of the second offense.[79] An equivalent state offense qualifies as a subsection 3559(e) predicate when it consists of conduct that would be a federal offense should it occur under one of two jurisdictional circumstances—(1) the offense involves use of the mails or interstate commerce, or (2) the offense occurs on a federal enclave, prison, or facility, or in Indian country.[80] Although the predicate state offense must be committed against a child, the victim's status as a child need not be an element of the state offense.[81] Moreover, the state predicate offense need have no federal nexus at the time of commission; it is enough that it would have been a federal offense under the designated jurisdictional circumstances.[82]

A qualified defendant must be sentenced under subsection 3559(e), notwithstanding the fact that he might otherwise have been sentenced under the less severe recidivist provisions of 18 U.S.C. 2551(e).[83]

Subsection 3559(e) provides defendants with a narrow affirmative defense when either the offense of conviction or the predicate offense arises under subsection 2422(b)(relating to inducing another to engage in prostitution) or under subsection 2423(a)(relating to transportation of a child for illicit sexual purposes). To claim the benefits of the defense, an accused must show by clear and convincing evidence that "(A) the sexual act or activity was consensual and not for the purpose of commercial or pecuniary gain; (B) the sexual act or activity would not be punishable by more than one year in prison under the law of the State in which it occurred; or (C) no sexual act or activity occurred."[84]

Restitution

The victims of the sexual abuse and sexual contact offenses punishable by mandatory minimum terms of imprisonment under chapter 109A are entitled to restitution.[85] As a general rule, federal courts may not order restitution absent express statutory authority.[86] Congress, however, has authorized the courts to order restitution for the victims of a wide range of federal crimes.[87] Moreover, section 2248 of chapter 109A demands that victims be compensated for "full amount" of the losses attributed to the offense, including an even more extensive array of expenses than might be available under the general provisions.[88] When the victim is a child, coverage extends to costs incurred by a child's parents "acting in their capacity as [such and] incurred as a result of [the] offense."[89]

Supervised Release

Federal courts may impose a term of supervised release at the time of sentencing.[90] They will do so in most serious sex offense cases.[91] Supervised release is not unlike parole, except that supervision is imposed in addition to, rather than in lieu of, time served in prison.[92] For most federal crimes, the maximum term of supervised release is no more than 5 years.[93] For the mandatory minimum sentencing offenses of chapter 109A and other serious federal sex offenses, the term of supervised release is "any term of years not less than 5, or life."[94] The court may sentence the offender to an additional term of imprisonment for failure to comply with the terms imposed as a condition of supervised release.[95]

If the court elects to issue a supervised release order, the order must require offenders to (1) refrain from criminal activity; (2) comply with sex offender registration requirements; (3) cooperate with authorized collection of DNA samples; and (4) submit to periodic drug tests.[96] The court also enjoys the discretion to impose any condition that is reasonably related to the statutory sentencing factors; that "involves no greater deprivation of liberty than is reasonably necessary"; and that is consistent with the Sentencing Commission's policy statements.[97] The courts regularly select conditions from among the Sentencing Guidelines' collection of close to 30 "standard," "special," or "additional" discretionary conditions in U.S.S.G. §5D1.3.[98]

The Sentencing Guidelines note that in sex offense cases "a condition[,] limiting the use of a computer or an interactive computer service in cases in which the defendant used such items," may be appropriate.[99] Nevertheless, the courts are divided over the extent to which a defendant's Internet use may be restricted in light of his conviction or past history.[100]

Sentencing courts may impose other supervisory release conditions as long as they satisfy the same criteria as those listed in the Sentencing Guidelines' collection: relatedness to statutory sentencing factors; no greater deprivation of liberty than necessary; and consistency with the Sentencing Guidelines' policy statements.[101] In case of sex offense convictions, the courts often limit the defendant's access to children following his release from prison. Some conditions restrict access to children generally;[102] some to areas frequented by children;[103] and some to occupations that involve frequent contact with children.[104] Whether these conditions survive review depends upon whether they are sufficiently related to the circumstances of the offense or the offender; whether they are drawn with sufficient precision to avoid undue restrictions on the defendant's liberty; and whether they are compatible with the policies of the Sentencing Guidelines.[105]

TRAVEL AND COMMERCE

Several mandatory minimum sentencing statutes punish sexual misconduct based on Congress's legislative authority to regulate interstate and foreign commerce. Most are found in chapter 117 (relating to transportation for illegal sexual activity), but a few others appear in either chapter 109A (relating to sexual abuse) or chapter 77 (relating to peonage, slavery, and human trafficking).

Chapter 117

Generally known as the Mann Act or the White Slave Act or the White Slave Traffic Act,[106] chapter 117 has five sections that proscribe travel or the use of the facilities of interstate or foreign commerce when they relate to sexual misconduct: (1) 18 U.S.C. 2421 that outlaws transporting or attempting to transport another in interstate or foreign commerce for purpose of prostitution or other illicit sexual activity; (2) 18 U.S.C. 2422 that outlaws either (a) enticing or attempting to entice another to engage such travel for such a purpose or (b) using or attempting to use the facilities of interstate commerce for such enticement of a minor for such purpose; (3) 18 U.S.C. 2423 that outlaws travel under various circumstances for illegal purposes; (4) 18 U.S.C. 2424 that outlaws false or incomplete filings relating to foreign nationals maintained in a house of prostitution; and (5) 18 U.S.C. 2425 that outlaws the use of the facilities of interstate commerce to communicate information relating to a juvenile for illicit sexual purposes. Sections 2422 and 2423 contain mandatory minimum sentencing provisions; the others do not.

Coercion and Enticement

Subsection 2422(b) requires imposition of a fine and a mandatory minimum term of imprisonment of 10 years for using the facilities of interstate commerce to coerce or entice a child under 18 years of age to engage in prostitution or other illicit sexual activity.[107] Subsection 2422(a) punishes such misconduct involving an adult victim with imprisonment for not more than 20 years with no minimum sentence required.

Coercion or enticement in violation of subsection 2422(b) consists of "(1) use of a facility of interstate commerce (2) to knowingly persuade, induce, entire, or coerce (3) an individual under the age of 18 (4) to engage in illegal sexual activity."[108] The subsection also proscribes any attempt to engage in such conduct.[109] Conviction for attempt requires proof of an intent to violate the subsection and of a substantial step beyond mere preparation towards accomplishment of that intent.[110] The intent required is the intent to entice or coerce—not the intent to engage in the illicit sexual act.[111] The effort to entice need not be addressed to a child directly; culpability may result from efforts to entice through an adult intermediary.[112] An offender who is misled as to the existence of an actual child victim is no less culpable.[113]

Convictions under subsection 2422(b) have withstood a number of constitutional challenges. Defendants have generally been unable establish that they have been exposed to grossly disproportionate sentences in violation of the Eighth Amendment;[114] or suffered a Fifth Amendment deprivation of due process in the form of entrapment,[115] the loss of judicial sentencing discretion,[116] or the denial of equal protection;[117] or lost First Amendment freedom by exposure to vague and overbroad laws;[118] or fallen victim to an constitutional violation of separation of powers.[119]

Transportation of a Minor

Section 2423 establishes four sex-related travel offenses and condemns attempts or conspiracies to commit them as well. Subsection 2423(a), which bans interstate or foreign transportation a child under 18 years of age for criminal sexual purposes, carries a mandatory minimum sentence of imprisonment of 10 years;[120] the same mandatory minimum applies to attempts or conspiracies to violate the subsection.[121] The other three subsections—travel for illicit sexual purposes; travel and illicit sexual conduct overseas; and facilitation of travel for illicit sexual purposes—punish violations by imprisonment for not more than 30 years, with no minimum term of imprisonment required.[122]

"To obtain a conviction under §2423(a), the government must prove beyond a reasonable doubt that the defendant: (1) knowingly transported a minor across state lines, (2) with the intent to engage in sexual activity with the minor, and (3) that the minor was under eighteen at the time of the offense."[123] The government need not show that the defendant knew the minor was underage.[124] Nor must it show that illicit sexual activity was the sole purpose or even the dominant purpose for the travel, as long as it constituted a significant consideration.[125]

Travel to Sexually Abuse a Child

The Mann Act's prohibitions on an offender's travel for illicit sexual purposes carry no mandatory minimum penalties. However, chapter 109A, which ordinarily deals with prison and territorial offenses, provides for such a penalty. As noted earlier, subsection 2241(c) establishes a mandatory minimum sentence of imprisonment of not less than 30 years for "[w]hoever crosses a State line with intent to engage in a sexual act with a person who has not attained the age of 12 years ... or attempts to do so."[126] Recidivists face a mandatory term of life imprisonment.[127] Subsection 2241(d) provides that the government need not establish that the defendant knew that the victim was underage.[128]

Commercial Sex Trafficking of a Child or by Force

Section 1591 of chapter 77 establishes a pair of mandatory minimum sentencing provisions when commercial sex trafficking occurs in or affecting interstate or foreign commerce or within the special maritime or territorial jurisdiction of the United States. One outlaws sex trafficking; the other profiting from it.[129] In either case, violations are punishable by a fine and imprisonment for not less than 10 years, if the child is between the ages of 14 and 18 and no force or coercion is involved.[130] Otherwise, violations are punishable by a fine and imprisonment for not less than 15 years.[131]

Parsed to their elements the two offenses provide:

I.

(1) Whoever

(2) (A) in or affecting interstate or foreign commerce, or
  (B) within the special maritime and territorial jurisdiction of the United States,

(3) knowingly

(4) (A) recruits,
  (B) entices,
  (C) harbors,
  (D) transports,
  (E) provides,
  (F) obtains, or
  (G) maintains by any means

(5) a person;

(6) (A) knowing, or
  (B) in reckless disregard of the fact,

(7) that (A) means of force,
  (B) threats of force,
  (C) fraud,
  (D) coercion, or
  (E) any combination of such means

(8) (A) will be used to cause the person to engage in a commercial sex act, or

(B) (i) that the person has not attained the age of 18 years and
(ii) will be caused to engage in a commercial sex act....[132]

II.

(1) Whoever
(2) knowingly
(3) benefits
    (A) financially or
    (B) by receiving anything of value,
(4) from participation in a venture in which
    (A) a person was
    (B) (i) recruited,
        (ii) enticed,
        (iii) harbored,
        (iv) transported,
        (v) provided,
        (vi) obtained, or
        (vii) maintained by any means
    (C) (i) in or affecting interstate or foreign commerce, or
        (ii) within the special maritime and territorial jurisdiction of the United States,
(5) (A) knowing, or
    (B) in reckless disregard of the fact,
(6) that (A) means of force,
    (B) threats of force,
    (C) fraud,
    (D) coercion, or
    (E) any combination of such means
(7) (A) will be used to cause the person to engage in a commercial sex act, or
    (B) (i) that the person has not attained the age of 18 years and
        (ii) will be caused to engage in a commercial sex act....[133]

The courts have held that the interstate commerce prong of the two offenses comes within the reach of Congress's authority to regulate interstate and foreign commerce.[134] To pass muster, the defendant's misconduct must have at least some minimal effect on interstate or foreign commerce.[135] The prosecution, however, need not prove that the defendant knew that his activities were occurring in or affecting commerce.[136] Moreover, while as a general rule, the defendant must be shown to have known that his juvenile victim was underage,[137] the statute relieves the government of the obligation, if the defendant has had sufficient opportunity to observe the victim and thus presumably to discern the victim's age.[138]

Murder in the Course of Certain Sexual Offenses

Section 2245 establishes a mandatory minimum sentence of imprisonment for any term of years for murder committed during the course of a violation of sex trafficking (18 U.S.C. 1591), child pornography (18 U.S.C. 2251, 2251A, 2260), or Mann Act violations (18 U.S.C. 18 U.S.C. 2421, 2422, 2423, 2425), regardless of the age of the victim.[139] Other sections of the Code establish a mandatory minimum term of life imprisonment for murder in the course of the other federal sex offenses, that is, those committed while in federal custody or within the special maritime or territorial jurisdiction of the United States.[140] Section 2251 establishes a 30-year mandatory minimum term of imprisonment when the production of, attempted production of, or conspiracy to produce, child pornography results in a death.[141]

Restitution and Supervised Release

Victims of sex trafficking are entitled to restitution under a specifically tailored provision available for the benefit of any victim of a violation of chapter 77.[142] The provision, section 1593, is comparable in some respects to section 2248 that applies in enclave cases. It too incorporates the compatible general restitution procedures.[143] It uses essentially the same "legal guardian" language.[144] Thus, coverage presumably extends to parental costs incurred on behalf of a victimized child.[145] It calls for restitution in the full amount of the victim's losses.[146] It references a similar list of specific qualifying expenses, but adds to the list the right to recover the value of the services of the trafficked victim.[147]

The Mann Act contains no explicit restitution provision. Some offenders may also be guilty of sex trafficking or some sex offense that triggers a crime-specific restitution requirement.[148] If not, the court must order offenders to pay victim restitution under the general restitution provisions of 18 U.S.C. 3663A.[149]

As in the case of chapter 109A, offenders convicted of Mann Act violations or sex trafficking must be sentenced to a term of supervised release for "any term of years not less than 5, or life."[150] The mandatory conditions for supervised release demand that the defendant: (1) comply with sex offender registration requirements; (2) submit to collection of DNA samples; (3) agree to periodic drug testing; and (4) refrain from engaging in criminal activity.[151] The court may impose any discretionary conditions that relate to the statutory sentencing factors concerning the offense or the offender; that are consistent with Sentencing Guidelines policies; and that do not unduly restrict the defendant's liberty.[152] As noted earlier, the courts often condition a sex offender's supervised release on restricted use of the Internet and limited contact with children.[153]

CHILD PORNOGRAPHY

Four federal child pornography sections establish mandatory minimum terms of imprisonment for violations: 18 U.S.C. 2251 (relating to sexual exploitation of children), 18 U.S.C. 2251A (relating to selling or buying children), 18 U.S.C. 2252 (relating to certain activities relating to material involving sexual exploitation of children), and 18 U.S.C. 2252A (relating to certain activities relating to material constituting or containing child pornography).

Production of Child Pornography

Section 2251 creates a series of mandatory minimum terms of imprisonment for the production of, attempted production of, and conspiracy to produce, child pornography or related misconduct under various jurisdictional circumstances. First time offenders are punishable by a fine and imprisonment for not less than 15 years; offenders with a prior conviction face a fine and imprisonment for not less than 25 years; and offenders with 2 or more prior convictions must be fined and sentenced to imprisonment for at least 35 years.[154] Should a death result from the commission of such offense, the offender must be imprisoned for at least 30 years.[155]

Section 2251 outlaws four substantive offenses: the use of a child to produce child pornography, subsection 2251(a); the participation of a parent or other custodian of a child in such production, subsection 2251(b); the overseas production of such material, subsection 2251(c); and the advertising of such material, subsection 2251(d). Subsection 2251(e) applies the same penalties to attempts or conspiracies to commit any of the four substantive offenses.

The elements common to all four are a child under 18 years of age[156] and at least the goal of creating a visual depiction of sexually explicit conduct of the child.[157] A majority of courts have held that neither the statute nor the Constitution requires the prosecution to show that the defendant knew the child was underage and that mistake of age constitutes no defense.[158]

"Visual depiction" includes photographs, video, and computer disks.[159] "Sexually explicit conduct" is defined to encompass various sexual acts as well as "lascivious exhibition[s]" of an individual's pubic area.[160] The lower federal appellate courts have endorsed the so-call *Dost* factors as a guide to determine when the otherwise lawful depiction of nudity has become a lascivious exhibition.[161]

Subsection 2251(a): Use of a Child to Produce

Subsection 2251(a) outlaws employment, use, or inducement of a child to produce a visual depiction of sexually explicit conduct under a range of jurisdictional circumstances, or by virtue of subsection (e) attempting or conspiring to do so.[162] The jurisdictional circumstances include interstate or territorial transportation of the child, anticipated or actual transmission or transportation of the depiction in or affecting interstate commerce, and use of materials transported in interstate commerce.[163] The courts have held that subsection 2251(a) constitutes a valid exercise of Congress's legislative power under the commerce clause.[164] Moreover, they have concluded that its mandatory minimum term of imprisonment does not offend the Eighth Amendment's prohibition against cruel and unusual punishments.[165]

Subsection 2251(b): Permitting the Use of a Child to Produce

Subsection 2251(b) applies the mandatory minimums of subsection 2251(e) to a parent, or other custodian of a child under 18 years of age, who permits, attempts to permit, or conspires to permit a child to be used for the visual depiction of sexually explicit conduct under jurisdictional circumstances comparable to those that apply to subsection 2251(a).[166] A related provision with a more substantial mandatory minimum sentence of imprison appears in

18 U.S.C. 2251A and differs primarily in its requirement of a transfer of custody or control.[167]

Subsection 2251(c): Overseas Production

Subsection 2251(c) applies the mandatory minimums of subsection 2251(e) to the overseas use, attempted use, or conspiracy to use, a child in the visual depiction of sexually explicit conduct with the intent to transport, or the transportation of, the depiction into the United States.[168]

Subsection 2251(d): Advertising

Subsection 2251(d) applies the mandatory minimums of subsection 2251(e) to anyone who "knowingly makes, prints, or publishes, or causes to be made, printed, published any notice or advertisement seeking or offering child pornography"[169] or to anyone seeking or offering to participate in the production of child pornography under various jurisdictional circumstances.[170] Federal jurisdiction exists if the notice or advertisement is transported or transmitted using the facilities of interstate commerce or the defendant anticipates that it will be.[171] The notice or advertisement need not "specifically state that it offers or seeks a visual depiction to violate §2251(c)(1)(A);" all that is required is that its implications are clear.[172]

Selling or Buying Children for Pornographic Purposes

Section 2251A demands a mandatory minimum sentence of imprisonment of 30 years for those convicted of relinquishing or acquiring custody or control of a child under 18 years of age knowing or intending that the child will be used to produce visual depictions of sexually explicit conduct, under certain jurisdictional circumstances.[173]

"Custody or control" is statutorily defined to "include[] temporary supervision over or responsibility for a minor whether legally or illegally obtained."[174] "The statute does not require transfer of full parental authority; something less than the control a parent exercises—including ... limitations on time and scope—suffices to violate the law."[175] Moreover, "the terms contained in the title of §2251A(b)—buying and selling—do not exclusively define the statute's reach."[176] The statute's reach extends as well to instances where the defendant acquires custody or control of the child by paying the victim herself.[177]

Federal jurisdiction over the offense exists if it occurred within the territorial jurisdiction of the United States, if it involved travel in or affecting interstate commerce, or if the offer was transported or transmitted through the facilities in or affecting interstate commerce.[178]

Certain Activities Involving Child Pornography (Real Child)

Three of the four offenses created in 18 U.S.C. 2252 require imposition of a sentence of imprisonment for not less than 5 years: transportation, receipt, or possession with intent to sell, of visual depictions of sexually explicit conduct involving a child under 18 years of age—under various jurisdictional circumstances.[179] Attempts or conspiracies to commit those offenses carry the same mandatory minimum penalties.[180] Simple possession by a first time offender is not punishable by a mandatory minimum term of imprisonment.[181] Defendants charged with any of the four offenses, who have a prior similar conviction, face increased mandatory minimum sentences of imprisonment.[182]

Transporting

The mandatory minimum sentences of subsection 2252(b)(1) apply to those convicted of violating subsection 2252(a)(1) which outlaws the transportation or transmission of child pornography in or affecting interstate commerce or by using the facilities of interstate commerce.[183] The mandatory minimum sentences apply as well to those convicted of attempting or conspiring to violate the subsection.[184]

"Under Section 2252(a)(1), the government must prove that: (1) the defendant knowingly transported or shipped, (2) in interstate or foreign commerce, (3) any visual depiction involving the use of a minor engaging in sexually explicit conduct."[185] The government must also prove that the visual depiction was of an actual child not a mere computer simulation,[186] and that the defendant knew the child was underage.[187]

Moreover, simply because the statute indicates that transportation may take the form of computer transmission "does not mean that use of a computer is a required element of the crime."[188]

For purposes of subsection 2252(a)(1), "interstate commerce" includes commerce to and from the possessions and the territories of the United States, and "foreign commerce" includes travel between foreign nations by way of the United States.[189] The government, however, need not prove that the defendants know of the interstate or foreign commercial nature of the transportation or shipment.[190]

When the government seeks the 15-year recidivist mandatory minimum sentence and the "state law [upon which the prior conviction was based] covers conduct some of which is within, and the rest of which is outside, the scope of a recidivist statute, the federal court may examine the [state] charging papers (and any guilty-plea colloquy) to classify the conviction."[191]

Receipt or Distribution

The same mandatory minimum terms of imprisonment apply when the defendant is convicted of receipt or distribution of, attempted receipt or distribution of, or conspiracy to receive or distribute, child pornography, under the same jurisdictional circumstances—not less than 15 years with a prior conviction; not less than 5 years otherwise.[192]

"The elements of receipt under 18 U.S.C. 2252(a)(2) require the defendant to knowingly receive an item of child pornography, and the item to be transported in interstate or foreign commerce" or otherwise satisfy the subsection's jurisdictional requirements.[193]

> To be sure, the exact contours of the crime of "knowingly receiving" electronic child pornography in a constantly shifting technological background are murky. Part of the problem is that computers connected to the internet store vast quantities of data about which many users know nothing. As a user browses the internet, the computer stores images and text and other kinds of data in its temporary memory the way a ship passing through the ocean collects barnacles that cling to its hull. Thus, there is some risk that the computer of an internet user not intending to access child pornography may be infected with child pornography. Understandably, our sister circuits have struggled with whether to impute knowledge from the presence of illicit files found in such temporary storage.[194]

Ultimately, the facts of a given case will determine whether the defendant is the unwitting victim of technology or knowingly received child pornography.[195] The government's burden includes proving that the defendant knew that child depicted was real and underage.[196]

For purposes of the jurisdictional element, "the government prove[s] images traveled interstate when it introduce[s] evidence that the defendant received images that were transmitted over the Internet."[197]

To be guilty of attempted violation of subsection 2252(b)(2), the defendant must have intended to receive or distribute child pornography and taken a substantial step towards the achievement of that goal.[198]

When a court faces the question of whether a defendant must be sentenced to the mandatory minimum 15-year term of imprisonment reserved for recidivists in a case where the prior conviction occurred under a statute proscribing both qualifying and non-qualifying offenses, the court "may refer to the charging document, the terms of a plea agreement, the transcript of the colloquy, jury instructions, and other comparable judicial records."[199]

Sale or Possession with Intent to Sell

Subsection 2252(a)(3), which prohibits the sale of, or possession with intent to sell, child pornography under various jurisdiction circumstances, requires imposition of a 5-year mandatory minimum term of imprisonment as well (a minimum of 15 years for recidivists).[200] The same penalties must be assessed upon conviction of an attempt or conspiracy to violate the subsection.[201] Jurisdiction exists if the offense occurs within the special maritime and territorial jurisdiction of the United States, on a federal facility or Indian reservation.[202] It also exists if interstate commerce is implicated in the offense.[203]

Recidivist Possession

Recidivists in possession of child pornography must be sentenced to 10-year minimum term of imprisonment under subsection 2252(a)(4), as must a recidivist convicted of attempting or conspiring to violate the subsection.[204] The necessary jurisdictional circumstances are the same as those which apply in the case of the sale offense under subsection 2252(a)(3).[205]

Qualifying prior convictions may include convictions under either state or federal law.[206] The offender's prior state conviction must be "related to" one of the statutorily described offenses and involve a minor, but the statute of conviction need not list a minor victim as an element of the offense.[207] "[T]he sentencing court looks to the fact of conviction and the statutory definition of the prior offense and determines whether the full range of conduct encompassed by the statute qualifies to enhance the sentence."[208] In this exercise, "[i]f the statute [of prior conviction] criminalizes both conduct that would qualify a defendant for an enhancement, as well as conduct that would not do so, the court may refer to the charging document, the terms of a plea agreement, the transcript of the colloquy, jury instructions, and the comparable judicial records to determine the basis for the guilty plea or verdict [in the prior case]."[209]

Subsection 2252(a)(4) has two distinctive features. First, offenders are not subject to a mandatory minimum term of imprisonment, unless the recidivist provisions are tripped.[210] Second, subsection 2252(c) provides a narrow explicit statutory defense, available when possession is minimal and the individual destroys the material or reveals it to authorities.[211]

Certain Activities Involving Child Pornography (Real and Virtual)

Sections 2252 and 2252A were almost identical at one point.[212] Section 2252 covered only visual depictions of sexual activity involving an actual child. Section 2252A covered visual depictions of sexual activity involving a digitally created child as well.[213] Other changes have occurred over the years, but that essential distinction remains. So too do the mandatory minimum terms of imprisonment that attend comparable violations of either section.

At least a 5-year term of imprisonment must be imposed for a violation, attempt to violate, or conspiracy to violate any of five child pornography-related offenses found in subsection 2252A: transportation; receiving or distributing; reproducing or promoting; selling or possession with intent to sell; or providing to a child.[214] Recidivists must be sentenced to imprisonment for not less than 15 years (not less than 10 years for a recidivist guilty of simple possession).[215] As discussed below, a 20-year mandatory term of imprisonment attends conviction for a child exploitation enterprise offense involving multiple violations of subsection 2252A(a) and related child abuse offenses that involve several children and several collaborators.[216]

Transporting

A 5-year mandatory term of imprisonment must be imposed on "[a]ny person who - (1) knowingly mails, or transports or ships using any means or facility of interstate or foreign commerce or in or affecting interstate or foreign commerce by any means, including by computer, any child pornography."[217] A mandatory 15-year term of imprisonment awaits recidivists.[218]

The subsection's recently expanded jurisdictional statement ("using any means ... affecting ... commerce") eliminates the split among the lower federal appellate courts over whether the earlier version of the statute covered any Internet use, or use where actual interstate transportation can be shown.[219] On the other hand, the use of a computer is not an element of the offense; the offense may be committed with or without the use of computer.[220]

Defendants accused of violating the transportation prohibition of subsection 2252A(a)(1) enjoy a relatively narrow affirmative defense.[221] The defense is available, if, after giving the required pre-trial notice, the defendant establishes that the alleged child pornography did not involve the use of a real child or the image of a real child.[222]

Receipt or Distribution

Section 2252A punishes the knowing receipt or distribution of child pornography, committed under certain jurisdictional circumstances, with imprisonment for not less than 5 years.[223] It punishes attempt and conspiracy in the same manner.[224] It imposes a minimum 15-year term of imprisonment upon recidivists.[225] The offense must be committed knowingly; inadvertent receipt is not a violation.[226] Knowing violation occurs, for instance, when the defendant "intentionally views, acquires, or accepts child pornography on a computer from an outside source."[227]

Attempted violation requires evidence of an intent to commit the offense and a substantial step beyond mere preparation towards that goal.[228] Factual impossibility, such as the absence of a real child in a sting situation, poses no obstacle to conviction for attempt.[229]

Possession of child pornography under subsection 2252A(a)(5) is a lesser included offense to the crime of receipt of child pornography under subsection 2252A(a)(2).[230] The Constitution's double jeopardy clause thus precludes punishment under both subsections for the same misconduct.[231] Punishment under both subsections is permissible, however, when each addresses a different violation.[232] The double jeopardy clause may also bar punishment for receipt of child pornography under both subsection 2252(a)(2) and 2252A(a)(2), unless the offenses involve different violations; for example, the 2252A(a)(2) offense involves a digital image and the other involves a real child.[233]

Reproduction or Promotion

Knowingly reproducing or promoting child pornography carries the same 5-year mandatory minimum term of imprisonment (15 years for recidivists).[234] Reproduction and the promotion offenses are distinct. Both offenses, however, rest on a broad claim of federal jurisdiction: utilization of a means or facility "affecting interstate or foreign commerce" by any manner "including by computer."[235]

The Supreme Court in *Williams* held that neither the reproduction nor promotion proscription violates either First Amendment over breadth restrictions or Fifth Amendment due process vagueness limitations.[236] The Court dissected several of subsection 2252A(a)(3)'s features in the course of its analysis.

First, it observed that the knowledge requirement applies to both the reproduction and promotion offenses.[237] Second, it said that the action elements of the promotion offense—"advertises, promotes, presents, distributes, or solicits"—bespeaks a transaction, although not necessarily a commercial transaction.[238] "That is to say, the statute penalizes speech that accompanies or seeks to induce a transfer of child pornography—via production or physical delivery—from one person to another."[239]

For the promotion offense, the advertisement, promotion, or presentation must be advanced with one of two intents: either "in a manner that reflects belief" that child pornography is being offered, or in a manner that is calculated to induce another to believe child pornography is being offered. As for the first, the manner of advertisement, promotion, or presentation "must objectively manifest a belief that the material is child pornography; a mere belief, without an accompanying statement or action that would lead a reasonable person to understand that the defendant holds that belief, is insufficient."[240] As for the second, "the defendant must 'intend' that the listener believe the material to be child pornography, and must select a manner of 'advertising, promoting, presenting, distributing, or soliciting' the material that he thinks will engender the belief—whether or not a reasonable person would think the same."[241]

Defendants charged with the reproduction offense may invoke the narrow affirmative defense covering pornography that involves only adults; defendants charged with the promotion offense may not.[242]

Sale or Intent to Sell

The same 5- and 15-year mandatory minimum terms of imprisonment follow conviction for selling or possession with intent to sell child pornography if committed under a wide range of jurisdictional circumstances, or for attempting or conspiring to do so.[243] Jurisdiction exists if the offense occurs on federal enclaves or facilities or in Indian country.[244] It also exists if the offense involves transportation using a means or facility in or affecting interstate or foreign commerce.[245] The affirmative defense available when children have not been used in the pornography may be claimed by defendants charged with selling or intent to sell child pornography.[246]

Offering Child Pornography to a Child

Section 2252A requires a fine and a minimum term of imprisonment of 5 years for offering child pornography to a child with the intent to induce the child to engage in illegal activity, or attempting or conspiring to do so.[247] It requires a fine and a minimum term of 15 years for recidivists.[248] The offense is punishable if the offer, the pornography, or the material used to produce the pornography, was transported using a means or facility in or affecting interstate or foreign commerce.[249] The defendants charged under the offering offense of subsection 2252A(a)(6) may not claim the affirmative defense available elsewhere for when the pornography involves only adults.[250]

Recidivist Possession

There is no mandatory minimum term of imprisonment for conviction of simple possession of child pornography.[251] However, there is a 10-year mandatory minimum term of imprisonment for conviction of possession by a recidivist.[252] The possession which triggers the minimum sentence may occur in Indian country or on federal enclaves or facilities.[253] Interstate commerce may also provide a basis for jurisdiction.[254] Defendants charged with possession may assert the affirmative, adults only pornography defense, if they do so in a timely fashion.[255]

Child Molesting Enterprises

Subsection 2252A(g) outlaws "child exploitation enterprises," a crime punishable by a fine and imprisonment "for any term of years not less than 20 or for life."[256] The crime's federal predicate felony offenses include not only pornography, but sex trafficking, kidnaping a child, sex abuse of a child, and Mann Act violations involving a child. More precisely, the penalty applies to:

(1) Whoever
(2) in concert with three or more other persons
(3) commits a series of predicate offenses

(4) constituting three or more separate incidents
(5) involving more than one victim
(6) when the predicate offenses involve felony violations of:
18 U.S.C. 1591 (relating to sex trafficking of a child or by force)
18 U.S.C. 1201 (relating to kidnaping of a child)
18 U.S.C. ch. 109A (relating to sexual abuse of a child)
18 U.S.C. ch. 110 (relating to pornography but not including record-keeping violations), or
18 U.S.C. ch. 117 (relating to sex offenses involving travel).[257]

Each predicate offense need not involve more than one victim nor be committed in concert with three other offenders; it is enough that the series of predicate offenses, taken in total involve more than one victim and three or more other offenders.[258] The Constitution's double jeopardy clause bars punishment for both a violation of subsection 2252A(g) and for conspiracy to violate the underlying predicate offenses.[259]

Restitution and Supervised Release

Child pornography offenses come with their own mandatory restitution provisions, not unlike those covering sex trafficking and sex abuse in federal enclaves.[260] The provision, section 2259, is much like section 2248 that applies in enclave cases. It adopts the procedures generally applicable in restitution cases.[261] Its definition of the term the "victim" suggests that parents must be awarded restitution for expenses incurred on behalf of a victimized child.[262] The examples of qualifying expenses are the same as those used for the victims of sexual abuse in federal enclaves under section 2248. It references a similar list of specific qualifying expenses, but adds to the list the right to recover the value of the services of the trafficked victim.[263]

Offenders convicted of a mandatory minimum pornography offense must be sentenced to a term of supervised release for "any term of years not less than 5, or life."[264] A defendant sentenced to a term of supervised release must (1) avoid further criminal activity; (2) submit to drug testing and the collection of DNA samples; and (3) obey sex offender registration requirements.[265] In addition, Internet use and child contact restrictions are particularly common conditions of supervised release in pornography cases.[266] Here too, however, the discretionary conditions of supervised release must be consistent the policies of the Sentencing Guidelines, must be related to the statutory sentencing factors concerning the circumstances of the offense and the offender, and must not unduly deprive the defendant of his liberty.[267]

Table 1. Federal Sex Offenses: Mandatory Minimum Terms of Imprisonment

Citation	Offense	Mandatory Minimum Term of Imprisonment
18 U.S.C. 2241(a)	aggravated sexual assault (by threat or force)(including attempt)	any term of years
18 U.S.C. 2241(b)	aggravated sexual assault (upon an incapacitated victim)(including attempt)	any term of years
18 U.S.C. 2241(c)	a. sexual act (victim under 12 or victim under 16 and at least 4 years the offender's junior)(including attempt) b. with a prior conviction	a. 30 years b. life
18 U.S.C. 1591	a. sex trafficking by force or fraud or of a child under 14 b. sex trafficking of a child (14 to 18)(w/o force or fraud)	a. 15 years b. 10 years
18 U.S.C. 2422(b)	enticing or coercing a child under 18 to engage in prostitution (including attempt)(Mann Act)	10 years
18 U.S.C. 2423(a)	transporting a child under 18 for illicit sexual purposes (including attempt) (Mann Act)	10 years
18 U.S.C. 2245	murder in the course of a Mann Act, sex trafficking, or production of child pornography offense	any term of years
18 U.S.C. 2251	child pornography: inducing a child under 18 to produce, custodial involvement in production, or advertising (including attempt) a. death results b. 2 or more prior convictions c. 1 prior conviction d. otherwise	a. 30 years b. 35 years c. 25 years d. 15 years
18 U.S.C. 2251A	child pornography: custodial involvement in production	30 years
18 U.S.C. 2252	a. child pornography (real): transportation, receipt, or sale (including attempt) b. prior conviction c. child pornography (real): recidivist possession	a. 5 years b. 15 years c. 10 years
18 U.S.C. 2252A	a. child pornography (real or virtual): transportation, receipt, promotion, sale, or distribution to a child (including attempt) b. prior conviction c. child pornography (real or virtual): recidivist possession	a. 5 years b. 15 years c. 10 years

Table 1. (Continued)

Citation	Offense	Mandatory Minimum Term of Imprisonment
18 U.S.C. 2252A(g)	child exploitation enterprise; 3 or more instances involve 3 or more others and multiple victims of child pornography, child sex trafficking, or Mann Act violations involving a child	20 years
18 U.S.C. 3559(e)	federal sex offense (sex trafficking, sexual assault, Mann Act, or production of child pornography violation), involving a victim under 17, by an offender with a prior federal or state equivalent conviction and sentence	life

End Notes

[1] For a general discussion of federal child sex abuse statutes, see CRS Report R42132, *Sexual Abuse of Children: Federal Criminal Offenses*, by Richard M. Thompson II.

[2] Act of April 30, 1790, 1 Stat. 112-15 (1790).

[3] Congress set the maximum term of imprisonment under the Sedition Act at five years and at three years under the Logan Act, Act of July 14, 1798, 1 Stat. 596 (1798) and the Act of January 30, 1799, 1 Stat. 613 (1799), respectively.

[4] Act of March 3, 1825, §4, 4 Stat. 115 (1825).

[5] Rev. Stat. §5345 (1878); Act of March 4, 1909, §278, 35 Stat. 1143 (1909); 18 U.S.C. 2031 (1946 ed. Supp. II).

[6] Protection of Children Against Sexual Exploitation Act of 1977, P.L. 95-225, §2(a), 92 Stat. 7 (1978).

[7] *18 U.S.C. 2241 (aggravated sexual assault)*: Sexual Abuse Act of 1986, P.L. 99-646, §87(b), 100 Stat. 3620 (1986).*18 U.S.C. 2251A (buying and selling a child for pornographic production)*: Child Pornography and Obscenity Enforcement Act of 1988, Title VII N of the Anti-Drug Abuse Act of 1988, P.L. 100-690, §7512(a), 102 Stat. 4486(1988).

18 U.S.C. 2245 (federal sex offenses resulting in death): Federal Death Penalty Act of 1994, Title VI, of the Violent Crime Control and Law Enforcement Act of 1994, P.L. 103-322, §60010(a)(2), 108 Stat. 1972 (1994).

18 U.S.C. 2252A (child pornography (real and virtual): Child Pornography Prevention Act of 1996, Div. A, Title I, of the Act Making Omnibus Consolidated Appropriations for the Fiscal Year Ending September 30, 1997, and for Other Purposes, P.L. 104-208, §101(a), 110 Stat. 3009-28 (1996).

18 U.S.C. 3559(e)(mandatory life imprisonment for repeat sex offenders): Protection of Children from Sexual Predators Act of 1988), P.L. 105-314, §501, 112 Stat. 2980 (1998).

18 U.S.C. 1591(sex trafficking): Trafficking Victims Protection Act of 2000, §112(a), P.L. 106-386, 114 Stat. 1487(2000).

18 U.S.C. 2422(b)(enticement to child prostitution), 2423(a)(travel to engage in illicit sexual purposes): Prosecutorial Remedies and Other Tools to End the Exploitation of Children Today Act (PROTECT Act) of 2003, §§103(a)(2)(B),(a)(2)(C), P.L. 108-21, 117 Stat. 653 (2003).

18 U.S.C. 2242 (sexual abuse): Adam Walsh Child Protection and Safety Act of 2006, §§205, 207(2), P.L. 109-248 120 Stat. 613, 615 (2006).

[8] United States Sentencing Commission, Results of Survey of United States District Court Judges, January 2010 through March 2010, Question 1 (June 2010), available at http://www.ussc.gov/Research/Research_Projects/Surveys/20100608_judge_Survey.pdf.

[9] United States Sentencing Commission, *Mandatory Minimum Penalties in the Federal Criminal Justice System* (*2011Report*), 365 (October 2011), available at http://www.ussc.gov.

[10] *Id.* at 369.

[11] This is the only one of the three that the Sentencing Commissions report identifies as having a mandatory minimum sentencing provision. *Id.* at A-8.

[12] The conclusion is doubtful because it requires the phrase "any" term of years to include a term of "no" years. As the Supreme Court has said that the term "any" refers to each member or group of members of a class, that is, "read naturally, the word 'any' has an expansive meaning, that is, 'one of some indiscriminately of whatever kind,'" *ALI v. Federal Bureau of Prisons*, 552 U.S. 214, 219 (2008). Thus, "any" can be read to mean "'all' things.... Specifically, 'any thing' means quite literally 'any thing whatever, something, no matter what," *United States v. Townsend*, 630 F.3d1003, 1011 (11th Cir. 2011).

Besides, the courts have been equally clear that construction often depends on context. *United States v. Alvarez-Sanchez*, 511 U.S. 350, 357 (1994)(emphasis in the original)("Because the statute applies to persons in the custody of '*any*' law enforcement officer or law enforcement agency, respondent suggests that the §3501(c) 6-hour time period begins to run whenever a person is arrested by local, state, *or* federal officers. We believe respondent errs in placing dispositive weight on the broad statutory reference to 'any' law enforcement officer or agency without considering the rest of the statute"). The phrase "any term of years" is a sentencing option reserved for most serious federal crimes—murder, kidnaping, rape, 18 U.S.C. 1111, 2241, 1201. In addition, Congress has specifically declared that upon conviction for one of these crimes no court may sentence a defendant to probation rather than imprisonment. (18 U.S.C.3561(a)("A defendant who has been found guilty of an offense may be sentenced to a term of probation unless—(1) the offense is a Class A or Class B felony ..."). A Class A felony is one for which the maximum penalty is life imprisonment, or for which the maximum penalty is death; a Class B felony is one for which the maximum penalty is imprisonment for 25 years or more, 18 U.S.C. 3559(a)(1), (2).) It seems unlikely that Congress intended to permit a court to forgo a sentence of imprisonment in such cases, as long as it did not impose probation.

[13] *United States v. Rowe*, 414 F.3d 271, 280 (2d Cir. 2005)("In *United States v. Pabon-Cruz*, 391 F.3d 86 (2d Cir. 2004), we vacated the defendant's sentence and remanded for resentencing after holding that a violation of §2251(c)did not require imposition of a 10-year mandatory minimum sentence. As worded when Mr. Pabon-Cruz was prosecuted, §2251(c)'s penalty provision stated that violators 'shall be fined under this title *or* imprisoned not less than10 years nor more than 20 years, *and both*.' 18 U.S.C. 2251(d) (emphasis supplied). This same language applied when Rowe committed his crime. As we observed, 'the "and both" language ... makes no sense as a matter of grammar, usage, or law.... ' 391 F.3d at 105. Accordingly, we held that the District Court had the discretion to sentence defendant to either a fine or a term of imprisonment of not less than ten years or both. Because this was not clear to the parties or to the District Court at the time of sentencing, we are required to vacate the sentence and remand the cause to the District Court for resentencing consistent with our opinion here and with such Sentencing Guidelines as may be applicable in the circumstances presented"); *United States v. Rast*, 293 F.3d 735, 738, 739 (4th Cir. 2002)("This brings us back to the peculiar structure of §2251(d), which allows a fine in lieu of imprisonment, but requires a term of 'not less than 10 years' if imprisonment is imposed at all.... Section 2251(d) means just what Congress intended it to say: a district court may impose either a fine *or* imprisonment of not less than ten nor more than twenty years, or both").

[14] Although the Sentence Guidelines are advisory, a sentencing court must begin the sentence process by calculating the sentencing range recommended by the Guidelines, *Gall v. United States*, 552 U.S. 38, 49 (2007). The sentencing range for the base offense level of a violation of subsection 2241(a) begins at imprisonment for twelve years and seven months, U.S.S.G. §2A3.1, ch. 5 (Sentencing Table). A sentence will be upheld on appeal, if it is procedurally and substantively reasonable, *Gall v. United States*, 552 U.S. at 51. A sentence is procedurally reasonable, if it is free procedural defects such as the failure to properly calculate the recommended sentencing range under the Guidelines, *id.* A sentence is substantively reasonable, if it is appropriate "tak[ing] into account the totality of the circumstances, including the extent to any variance from the Guidelines range," *id.*

[15] *United States v. Lopez*, 514 U.S. 549 (1995).

[16] U.S. Const. Amend. X.

[17] U.S. Const. Art.I, §8, cl.18; see generally *United States v. Comstock*, 130 S.Ct. 1949 (2010).

[18] U.S. Const. Art.I, §8, cls.10, 17, 14, 3, and 18 respectively.

[19] E.g., 18 U.S.C. 2241(a)("Whoever, in the special maritime and territorial jurisdiction of the United States ... knowing causes another person to engage in a sexual act—(1) by using force against that other person ... shall be ... imprisoned for any term of years or life ...").

[20] E.g., 18 U.S.C. 2251(a), (e)("(a) Any person ... who transports any minor in or affecting interstate or foreign commerce ... with the intent that such minor engage in any sexually explicit conduct for the purpose of producing any visual depiction of such conduct.... (e) Any individual who violates ... this section shall be ... imprisoned not less than15 years ...").

[21] *United States v. Morrison*, 529 U.S. 598, 609 (2000)(internal citations omitted), quoting *United States v. Lopez*, 514 U.S. 549, 558-59 (1995).

[22] *Woodson v. North Carolina*, 428 U.S. 280, 305-306 (1976).

[23] *Ewing v. California*, 538 U.S. 11, 31-2 (2003); *Graham v. Florida*, 130 S.Ct. 2011, 2022-23 (2010). Although ordinarily not relevant in mandatory minimum sentencing cases, the Eighth Amendment also precludes punishment for the second category of cases, those involving crimes which Congress may not constitutional proscribe or those involving defendants it may not constitutionally punish, *id.* at 2222 ("The second classification of cases has used categorical rules to define Eight Amendment standards. The previous cases in this classification involved the death penalty. The classification in turn consists of two subsets, one considering the nature of the offense, the other considering the characteristics of the offender").

[24] *United States v. Brucker*, 646 F.3d 1012, 1018-19 (7th Cir. 2011)(10-year mandatory minimum sentence for attempting to entice a child to engage in sexual activity in violation of 18 U.S.C. 2422(b) did not constitute cruel and unusual punishment); *United States v. Hughes*, 632 F.3d 956, 959-60 (6th Cir. 2011)(same); *United States v. Malloy*,568 F.3d 166, 180 (4th Cir. 2009)(15-year mandatory minimum sentence for production of child pornography in violation of 18 U.S.C. 2251 did not constitute cruel and unusual punishment); *United States v. Polk*, 546 F.3d 74, 78(1st Cir. 2008)(same); *United States v. Meiners*, 485 F.3d 1211, 1213 (9th Cir. 2007)(15-year mandatory minimum sentence for advertising child pornography in violation of 2252A(a)(2) did not constitute cruel and unusual punishment).

[25] *Loving v. United States*, 517 U.S. 748, 757 (1996).

[26] *United States v. Chapman*, 500 U.S. 453, 467 (1991).

[27] *United States v. Brucker*, 646 F.3d 1012, 1019 (7th Cir. 2011)(18 U.S.C. 2422(b)(attempting to entice to commit a sexual act); *United States v. Hughes*, 632 F.3d 956, 962 (6th Cir. 2011)(same); *United States v. Paige*, 604 F.3d 1268, 1274 (11th Cir. 2010)(18 U.S.C. 2252A(child pornography)); *United States v. MacEwan*, 445 F.3d 237, 250-52 (3d Cir. 2006)(same).

[28] *Mistretta v. United States*, 488 U.S. 361, 412 (1989). Mistretta, sentenced under the guidelines to 18 months' imprisonment for conspiracy to distribute cocaine, argued that the guidelines constituted an unconstitutional delegation of Congress's legislative authority and that the service of judges upon the Commission constituted extrajudicial service at odds with the

separation of powers doctrine. The Court rejected both arguments concluding "that in creating the Sentencing Commission ... Congress neither delegated excessive legislative power nor upset the constitutionally mandated balance of powers among the coordinate Branches," *Id.* Prior to *Booker v. United States*, 543 U.S. 220 (2005), the Sentencing Guidelines were mandatory, 18 U.S.C. 3553(b)(1)(2000 ed.). If the Sentencing Guidelines called for imposition of a term of imprisonment, a sentencing court was bound to impose it, *id.*

[29] *United States v. Armstrong*, 517 U.S. 456, 464 (1996); U.S. Const. Amend. V ("No person shall ... be deprived of life, liberty, or property, without due process of law ..."); U.S. Const. Amend. XIV, §1 ("... [N]or shall any State ... deny to any person within its jurisdiction the equal protection of the laws").
The exercise of prosecutorial discretion on the basis of race offends equal protection, 517 U.S. at 464-65. In *Armstrong*, the defendant sought discovery in order to determine whether racial factors influenced the decision of which crack defendants should be tried in federal court and which should be left to the less severe jeopardy of state law. The Court held that in order to be entitled to discovery, a defendant must show that similarly situated offenders of other races were not prosecuted. *Id.*

[30] Cf., *Id.* at 464 ("One ... constraint, imposed by the equal protection component of the Due Process Clause of the Fifth Amendment ... is that the decision whether to prosecute may not be based on 'an unjustifiable standard such as race, religion, or other arbitrary classification'"); see also, *Heller v. Doe*, 509 U.S. 312, 320 (1993).

[31] *United States v. Brucker*, 646 F.3d 1012, 1018 (7th Cir. 2011)("That the federal defendant may face harsher punishment than his state counterpart, or vice verse, simply does not raise equal protection concerns"); *United States v. Hughes*, 632 F.3d 956, 961 (6th Cir. 2011)("Hughes points to several defendants who committed acts very similar to his—that is, they used the Internet to chat with undercover law enforcement officers masquerading as young girls, arranged meetings for the express purpose of sexual activity and were subsequently arrested and convicted. However, these defendants were not subject to the ten-year minimum sentence of §2422(b) because they were instead convicted under 18 U.S.C. §2423(b).... Section 2422 (b) essentially requires proof that the defendant attempted to communicate with the minor, and through that communication transform the minor into his victim. Section 2423(b) does not. The distinction is a rational basis on which Congress could have decided to punish the crimes differently"); *United States v. Nagel*, 559 F.3d 756, 760 (7th Cir. 2009)("Defendant's equal protection argument fails because criminal defendants who violate §2422(b) are not similarly situated for sentencing purposes with criminal defendants who violate the controlled substance offenses enumerated in §3553(f)").

[32] Cf., *United States v. Bass*, 536 U.S. 862, 863 (2002)("[A] defendant who seeks discovery of an [equal protection] claim of selective prosecution must show some evidence of both discriminatory effect and discriminatory intent").

[33] *United States v. DeMarce*, 564 F.3d 989, 1000 (8th Cir. 2009)("DeMarce argues that federal sexual abuse prosecutions have a disparate impact on Indians.... Congress intended to target sex offenders. The court concludes that the penalties associated with the Act serve the purpose of deterring sex offenders and are a rationally related to Congress's objective to protect children. See generally *United States v. Lemay*, 260 F.3d 1018, 1030 (9th Cir. 2001)(denying that changes to the Federal Rules of Evidence violated the equal protection rights of a Native American defendant); *United States v. McHorse*, 179 F.3d 889, 897 (10th Cir. 1999)(rejecting defendant's argument that federal sex crime prosecutions violated equal protection by disproportionately targeting Native Americans").

[34] "... [N]or shall any person be subject for the same offence to be twice put in jeopardy of life or limb...." U.S. Const. Amend.V; the double jeopardy clause is binding on the states through the due process clause of the Fourteenth Amendment, *Monge v. California*, 524 U.S. 721, 727 (1998).

[35] "No ... ex post facto law shall be passed...." U.S. Const. Art.I, §9. "No state shall ... pass any ... ex post facto law ..." U.S. Const. Art.I, §10.

[36] *Monge v. California*, 524 U.S. at 727-28.

[37] *California Dept. of Corrections v. Morales*, 514 U.S. 499, 504 (1995).

[38] See also, *Witte v. United States*, 515 U.S. 389, 400 (1995)("In repeatedly upholding such recidivism statutes, we have rejected double jeopardy challenges because the enhanced punishment imposed for the later offense is not to be viewed as either a new jeopardy or additional penalty for the earlier crimes, but instead as a stiffened penalty for the latest crime, which is considered to an aggravated offense because as repetitive one"); *United States v. Smith*, 581 F.3d 692, 695 (8th Cir. 2009).

[39] *Gryger v. Burke*, 334 U.S. 728, 732 (1948)("Nor do we think the fact that one of the convictions that entered into the calculations by which petitioner became a fourth offender occurred before the Act was passed, makes the Act invalidly retroactive...."); *United States v. Abraham*, 386 F.3d 1033, 1038 (11th Cir. 2004); *United States v. Springfiled*, 337 F.3d 1175, 1178 (10th Cir. 2003).

[40] See, e.g., 18 U.S.C. 2241(a)("Whoever, in the special maritime and territorial jurisdiction of the United States or in a Federal prison, or in any prison, institution, or facility in which persons are held in custody by direction of or pursuant to a contract or agreement with the head of any Federal department or agency, knowingly causes another person to engage in a sexual act ..."); a similar jurisdiction phrase occurs in each of chapter 109A's criminal provisions, 18 U.S.C. 2241(b), (c); 2242; 2243; 2244.

[41] 18 U.S.C. 7(3).

[42] *Jurisdiction Over Federal Areas Within the States: Report of the Interdepartmental Committee for the Study of Jurisdiction Over Federal Areas Within the States* (April 1956).

[43] 18 U.S.C. 7(9).

[44] 18 U.S.C. 3261-3267. Those employed by or accompanying the federal government are also subject to criminal liability for misconduct that would constitute a violation of chapter 77 (relating to peonage, slavery, and trafficking in persons) or chapter 117 (relating to transportation for illegal sexual purposes) if committed within the territorial jurisdiction of the United States, 18 U.S.C. 3271-3272.

[45] 18 U.S.C. 7(1), (2), (8). There is jurisdiction with respect to misconduct aboard an aircraft under comparable circumstances, 18 U.S.C. 7(5); 49 U.S.C. 46506.

[46] 18 U.S.C. 3299 ("Notwithstanding any other law, an indictment may be found or an information instituted at any time without limitation for any offense under section 1201 involving a minor victim, and for any felony under chapter109A, 110 (except for section 2257 and 2257A), or 117, or section 1591").

[47] *United States v. Gouveia*, 467 U.S. 180, 192 (1984), citing *United States v. Marion*, 404 U.S. 307, 322-24 (1971),and *United States v. Lovasco*, 431 U.S. 783, 788-90 (1977) ("[A]pplicable statutes of limitations protect against the prosecution's bringing stale criminal charges against any defendant, and, beyond that protection, the Fifth Amendment requires the dismissal of an indictment, even if it is brought within the statute of limitations, if the defendant can prove that the Government's delay in bringing the indictment was a deliberate device to gain an advantage over him and that it caused him actual prejudice in presenting his defense ").

[48] 18 U.S.C. 2241(a), (b).

[49] 18 U.S.C. 2241(c).

[50] 18 U.S.C. 2242. There is considerable overlap between section 2242 and subsection 2241(a) as well as subsection 2241(b).

[51] 18 U.S.C. 2244(b).

[52] 18 U.S.C. 3559(e).

[53] 18 U.S.C. 2246 ("As used in this chapter ... (2) the term 'sexual act' means - (A) contact between the penis and the vulva or the penis and the anus, and for purposes of this subparagraph contact involving the penis occurs upon penetration, however slight; (B)

contact between the mouth and the penis, the mouth and the vulva, or the mouth and the anus; (C) the penetration, however slight, of the anal or genital opening of another by a hand or finger or by any object, with an intent to abuse, humiliate, harass, degrade, or arouse or gratify the sexual desire of any person ...").

[54] 18 U.S.C. 2246 ("As used in this chapter ... (2) the term 'sexual act' means ... (D) the intentional touching, not through the clothing, of the genitalia of another person who has not attained the age of 16 years with an intent to abuse, humiliate, harass, degrade, or arouse or gratify the sexual desire of any person").

[55] 18 U.S.C. 2246 ("As used in this chapter . . (3) the term 'sexual contact' means the intentional touching, either directly or through the clothing, of the genitalia, anus, groin, breast, inner thigh, or buttocks of any person with an intent to abuse, humiliate, harass, degrade, or arouse or gratify the sexual desire of any person").

[56] 18 U.S.C. 2241("(a) By Force or Threat.—Whoever ... knowingly causes another person to engage in a sexual act (1) by using force against that other person; or (2) by threatening or placing that other person in fear that any person will be subjected to death, serious bodily injury, or kidnapping; or attempts to do so, shall be fined under this title, imprisoned for any term of years or life, or both. (b) By Other Means.—Whoever ... knowingly - (1) renders another person unconscious and thereby engages in a sexual act with that other person; or (2) administers to another person by force or threat of force, or without the knowledge or permission of that person, a drug, intoxicant, or other similar substance and thereby - (A) substantially impairs the ability of that other person to appraise or control conduct; and (B) engages in a sexual act with that other person; or attempts to do so, shall be fined under this title, imprisoned for any term of years or life, or both ...").

[57] *Id.* Federal crimes punishable by a maximum term of imprisonment of 1 year or more are classified as felonies, 18 U.S.C. 3559(a). Absent a specific countervailing provision, defendants convicted of a felony are subject to a fine of not more than $250,000 (not more than $500,000 for an organization), 18 U.S.C. 3571.

[58] *United States v. White Bull*, 646 F.3d 1082, 1087 (8th Cir. 2011).

[59] 18 U.S.C. 2241(c)("Whoever ... knowingly engages in a sexual act with another person who has not attained the age of 12 years, or knowingly engages in a sexual act under the circumstances described in subsections (a) and (b) with another person who has attained the age of 12 years but has not attained the age of 16 years (and is at least 4 years younger than the person so engaging), or attempts to do so, shall be fined under this title and imprisoned for not less than 30 years or for life. If the defendant has previously been convicted of another Federal offense under this subsection, or of a State offense that would have been an offense under either such provision had the offense occurred in a Federal prison, unless the death penalty is imposed, the defendant shall be sentenced to life in prison").

[60] *United States v. DeCoteau*, 630 F3d. 1091, 1097-98 (8th Cir. 2011).

[61] 18 U.S.C. 2241(c).

[62] *United States v. Robertson*, 606 F.3d 943, 953 (8th Cir. 2010); *United States v. DeMarce*, 564 F.3d 989, 998 (8th Cir. 2009).

[63] 18 U.S.C. 2241(d).

[64] *United States v. Juvenile Male*, 211 F.3d 1169, 1171-172 (9th Cir. 2000); *United States v. Ransom*, 942 F.2d 775, 776-78 (10th Cir. 1991).

[65] *United States v. Farley*, 607 F.3d 1294, 1336-345 (11th Cir. 2010).

[66] *United States v. DeMarce*, 564 F.3d 989, 1000 (8th Cir. 2009).

[67] *United States v. Robertson*, 606 F.3d 943, 951 (8th Cir. 2010).

[68] 18 U.S.C. 2242, 7(9), 3261-3267.

[69] 18 U.S.C. 2242.

[70] *Id.* ("Whoever, in the special maritime and territorial jurisdiction of the United States or in a Federal prison, or in any prison, institution, or facility in which persons are held in custody by direction of or pursuant to a contract or agreement with the head of any Federal department or agency, knowingly—(1) causes another person to engage in a sexual act by

threatening or placing that other person in fear (other than by threatening or placing that other person in fear that any person will be subjected to death, serious bodily injury, or kidnapping); or (2) engages in a sexual act with another person if that other person is—(A) incapable of appraising the nature of the conduct; or (B) physically incapable of declining participation in, or communicating unwillingness to engage in, that sexual act; or attempts to do so, shall be fined under this title and imprisoned for any term of years or for life").

[71] *United States v. Papakee*, 573 F.3d 569, 573-75 (intoxicated); *United States v. Fasthorse*, 639 F.3d 1182, 1184 (9th Cir. 2011)(asleep), citing *United States v. Smith*, 606 F.3d 1270, 1281 (10th Cir. 2010), and *United States v. Peters*, 277F.3d 963, 967-68 (7th Cir. 2002).

[72] *United States v. Betone*, 636 F.3d 384, 387-88 (8th Cir. 2011).

[73] 18 U.S.C. 2244.

[74] 18 U.S.C. 2244(a)(5)("Whoever, in the special maritime and territorial jurisdiction of the United States or in a Federal prison, or in any prison, institution, or facility in which persons are held in custody by direction of or pursuant to a contract or agreement with the head of any Federal department or agency, knowingly engages in or causes sexual contact with or by another person, if so to do would violate ... (5) subsection (c) of section 2241 of this title had the sexual contact been a sexual act, shall be fined under this title and imprisoned for any term of years or for life").

[75] 18 U.S.C. 2244.

[76] The defendant may be sentenced to death, if convicted of a capital offense, 18 U.S.C. 3559(e)(1).

[77] 18 U.S.C. 3559(e)(2)(D); *United States v. Doss*, 630 F.3d 1181, 1195 (9th Cir. 2011).

[78] 18 U.S.C. 3559(e)(2)(A).

[79] *Id.*

[80] 18 U.S.C. 3559(e)(2)(B)("[T]he term 'State sex offense' means an offense under State law that is punishable by more than one year in prison and consists of conduct that would be a Federal sex offense if, to the extent or in the manner specified in the applicable provision of this title - (i) the offense involved interstate or foreign commerce, or the use of the mails; or (ii) the conduct occurred in any commonwealth, territory, or possession of the United States, within the special maritime and territorial jurisdiction of the United States, in a Federal prison, on any land or building owned by, leased to, or otherwise used by or under the control of the Government of the United States, or in the Indian country (as defined in section 1151)").

[81] *United States v. Doss*, 630 F.3d 1181, 1197 (9th Cir. 2011).

[82] *United States v. Gallenardo*, 579 F.3d 1076, 1085-86 (9th Cir. 2009)("Gallenardo contends that his prior state conviction for felony sexual assault is not within 18 U.S.C. §3559(e)'s purview because his conduct did not involve interstate or foreign commerce.... the plain and unambiguous language of 18 U.S.C. §3559(e) undermines Gallenardo's argument. Section 3559(e)(2)(B) provides that a state sex offense qualifies as a predicate offense if the conduct 'would be' a Federal sex offense 'if it had involved interstate or foreign commerce' or 'if it occurred within federal jurisdiction'"); see also *United States v. Rosenbohm*, 564 F.3d 820, 823-25 (7th Cir. 2009).

[83] *United States v. Gallenardo*, 579 F.3d 1076, 1083-85 (9th Cir. 2009); *United States v. Moore*, 567 F.3d 187, 190-91 (6th Cir. 2009).

[84] 18 U.S.C. 3559(e)(3).

[85] 18 U.S.C. 2248 ("(a) In General. - Notwithstanding section 3663 or 3663A, and in addition to any other civil or criminal penalty authorized by law, the court shall order restitution for any offense under this chapter.... (b) ... (2) Enforcement. - An order of restitution under this section shall be issued and enforced in accordance with section 3664 in the same manner as an order under section 3663A ... (4) Order mandatory. - (A) The issuance of a restitution order under this section is mandatory. (B) A court may not decline to issue an order under this section because of - (i) the economic circumstances of the defendant; or (ii) the fact that

a victim has, or is entitled to, receive compensation for his or her injuries from the proceeds of insurance or any other source....").

[86] *United States v. Tsosie*, 639 F.3d 1213, 1219 (9th Cir. 2011); *United States v. Locke*, 643 F.3d 235, 246 (7th Cir. 2011); *United States v. Yielding*, 657 F.3d 688, 718 (8th Cir. 2011); *United States v. Brown*, 665 F.3d 1239, 1252 (11th Cir. 2011).

[87] 18 U.S.C. 3663-3664. See generally, CRS Report RL34138, *Restitution in Federal Criminal Cases*, by Charles Doyle.

[88] 18 U.S.C. 2248(b)(3)("For purposes of this subsection, the term 'full amount of the victim's losses' includes any costs incurred by the victim for - (A) medical services relating to physical, psychiatric, or psychological care; (B) physical and occupational therapy or rehabilitation; (C) necessary transportation, temporary housing, and child care expenses; (D) lost income; (E) attorneys' fees, plus any costs incurred in obtaining a civil protection order; and (F) any other losses suffered by the victim as a proximate result of the offense").

[89] 18 U.S.C. 2248(c)("For purposes of this section, the term 'victim' means the individual harmed as a result of a commission of a crime under this chapter, including, in the case of a victim who is under 18 years of age, incompetent, incapacitated, or deceased, the legal guardian of the victim or representative of the victim's estate, another family member, or any other person appointed as suitable by the court, but in no event shall the defendant be named as such representative or guardian"); *United States v. Tsosie*, 639 F.3d at 1220 ("This definition is not a model of legislative drafting. Nonetheless, it seems apparent enough that the purpose of the definition's reference to 'legal guardians' is to permit restitution of costs that legal guardians of minor victims, acting in their capacity as legal guardian, incurred as a result of an offense").

[90] 18 U.S.C. 3583(a)(emphasis added)("The court, in imposing a sentence to a term of imprisonment for a felony or a misdemeanor, may include as a part of the sentence a requirement that the defendant be placed on a term of supervised release *after imprisonment*, except that the court shall include as a part of the sentence a requirement that the defendant be placed on a term of supervised release if such a term is required by statute or if the defendant has been convicted for the first time of a domestic violence crime as defined in section 3561(b)"). See generally, CRS Report RL31653, *Supervised Release: A Brief Sketch of Federal Law*, by Charles Doyle, from which portions of this discussion are taken.

[91] Prior to *Booker v. United States*, 543 U.S. 220 (2005), the Sentencing Guidelines were mandatory. Then, federal courts had no alternative but to impose a term of supervised release following imposition of a mandatory minimum term of imprisonment of one or more, U.S.S.G. §5D1.1(a)(eff. November 1, 2004). The Guidelines now merely recommend supervised release in such cases, U.S.S.G. §5D1.1(a); *United States v. O'Georgia*, 569 F.3d 281, 288-89 (6th Cir. 2009). As the Supreme Court has made clear, Sentencing Guideline recommendations continue to carry great weight, *Gall v. United States*, 552 U.S. 38, 46-52 (2007).

[92] *Id.* See also, 18 U.S.C. 4205(a)(1982 ed.)("Whenever confined and serving a definite term or terms of more than one year, a prisoner shall be eligible for release on parole after serving one-third of such term or terms or after serving ten years of a life sentence or of a sentence of over thirty years ..."). The Sentencing Reform Act abolished parole for federal crimes committed after its effective date, P.L. 98-273, §218(a)(5), 98 Stat. 2027 (1984).

[93] 18 U.S.C. 3583(b).

[94] 18 U.S.C. 3583(k)(" Notwithstanding subsection (b), the authorized term of supervised release for any offense under section 1201 involving a minor victim, and for any offense under section 1591, 2241, 2242, 2243, 2244, 2245, 2250, 2251, 2251A, 2252, 2252A, 2260, 2421, 2422, 2423, or 2425, is any term of years not less than 5, or life").

[95] 18 U.S.C. 3583(e)("The court may ... (2) extend a term of supervised release if less than the maximum authorized term was previously imposed, and may modify, reduce, or enlarge the

conditions of supervised release, at any time prior to the expiration or termination of the term of supervised release, pursuant to the provisions of the Federal Rules of Criminal Procedure relating to the modification of probation and the provisions applicable to the initial setting of the terms and conditions of post-release supervision; (3) revoke a term of supervised release, and require the defendant to serve in prison all or part of the term of supervised release authorized by statute for the offense that resulted in such term of supervised release without credit for time previously served on postrelease supervision, if the court, pursuant to the Federal Rules of Criminal Procedure applicable to revocation of probation or supervised release, finds by a preponderance of the evidence that the defendant violated a condition of supervised release ... ; or (4) order the defendant to remain at his place of residence during nonworking hours and, if the court so directs, to have compliance monitored by telephone or electronic signaling devices, except that an order under this paragraph may be imposed only as an alternative to incarceration"). The term authorized by statute in the case of the mandatory minimum federal sex offenses is any term of years or life, 18 U.S.C. 3583(k).

[96] 18 U.S.C. 3583(d). The order of supervised release need only include a registration condition when the offender is otherwise required to register, *id.* Federal law requires any defendant convicted of any of the mandatory minimum sex offenses to register, 42 U.S.C. 16913(a), 16911.

[97] 18 U.S.C. 3583(d).

[98] E.g., U.S.S.G. §5D1.3(c), (d), (e)("The following 'standard' conditions are recommended for supervised release ... : (1) the defendant shall not leave the judicial district or other specified geographic area without the permission of the court or probation officer; (2) the defendant shall report to the probation officer as directed by the court or probation officer and shall submit a truthful and complete written report within the first five days of each month; ... (d) ... The following 'special' conditions of supervised release are recommended in the circumstances described and, in addition, may otherwise be appropriate in particular cases: (1) *Possession of Weapons* If the instant conviction is for a felony ... a condition prohibiting the defendant from possessing a firearm or other dangerous weapon. (2) *Debt Obligations* If an installment schedule of payment of restitution or a fine is imposed—a condition prohibiting the defendant from incurring new credit charges or opening additional lines of credit without approval of the probation officer unless the defendant is in compliance with the payment schedule.... (7) *Sex Offenses* If the instant offense of conviction is a sex offense ... (A) A condition requiring the defendant to participate in a program approved by the United States Probation Office for the treatment and monitoring of sex offenders. (B) A condition limiting the use of a computer or an interactive computer service in cases in which the defendant used such items ... (e) *Additional Conditions* ... The following 'special conditions' may be appropriate on a case-by-case basis: ... (4) *Occupational Restrictions* Occupational restrictions may be imposed as a condition of supervised release. <u>See</u> §5F1.5 (Occupational Restrictions)...").

[99] U.S.S.G. §5D1.3(d)(7)(B).

[100] *United States v. Miller*, 665 F.3d 114, 128-34 (5th Cir. 2011)(noting division among the circuits over whether Internet use may be conditioned on probation officer approval; over whether restrictions were only appropriate when use of the Internet was involved in commission of the offense; as well as over the permissible length and breadth of any restriction).

[101] 18 U.S.C. 3583(d).

[102] E.g., *United States v. Smith*, 655 F.3d 839, 843 (8th Cir. 2011)("The defendant shall have no contact, nor reside with children under the age of 18, including his/her own children, unless approved in advance by the U.S. Probation Officer in consultation with the treatment providers. The defendant must report all incidental contact with children to the U.S. Probation Officer and the treatment provider. Should the defendant have incidental contact

with a child, the defendant is required to immediately remove him/herself from the situation and notify his/her U.S. Probation Officer with[in] 24 hours of this contact"); *United States v. Albertson*, 645 F.3d 191, 194 (3d Cir. 2011)(comparable by permitting the defendant contact with his own children or with any child in the presence of an adult).

[103] E.g., *United States v. Thompson*, 653 F.3d 688, 692 (8th Cir. 2011)("Special condition 9 prohibits Thompson from 'access[ing] or com[ing] within 500 feet of schools, school yards, parks, arcades, playgrounds, amusement parks, or other places used primarily by children under the ages of 18 unless approved in advance by the U.S. Probation Officer"); *United States v. Musso*, 643 F.3d 566, 571 (7th Cir. 2011)(The defendant must "refrain from frequenting, loitering, or residing within 500 feet of locations where children congregate"); *United States v. Blinkinsop*, 606 F.3d 1110, 1119-120 (9th Cir. 2010)("Defendant shall not go to or loiter near schoolyards, parks, play grounds, arcades, or other p[l]aces primarily used by children under the age of 18").

[104] E.g., *United States v. Smith*, 655 F.3d at 844 ("The defendant shall not be employed in, or participate in, any volunteer activity that involves contact with children under the age of 18, except under circumstances approved in advance by the U.S. Probation Officer"); *United States v. Mike*, 632 F.3d 686, 691 (10th Cir. 2011)("[T]he defendant may not engage in an occupation where he has access to children without prior approval from his probation officer"); *United States v. Heckman*, 592 F.3d 400, 411 (3d Cir. 2010)("The defendant shall not obtain employment or perform volunteer work which includes, as part of his job/work description, contact with minor children").

[105] *United States v. Smith*, 655 F.3d at 846-47 ("The record does not, however, support Condition 6. Condition 6, a movement restriction, does not just ban loitering near protected places. Its 'not ... come within' language prohibits Smith even from driving by schools, parks, or other places used primarily by children, on main thoroughfares to legitimate activities.... Contrary to Smith's argument, 'no-contact' special conditions may be appropriate for other than child pornography convictions. Because Smith sexually abused a minor, and the probation officer may waive the condition, the district court acted within its discretion"); *United States v. Albertson*, 645 F.3d at 200 ("Albertson claims there is no support in the record for imposing a prohibition on associating with minors under age 18 (except his family).... At the time of his sentencing, Albertson had been charged with, among other things, indecent assault of his then-13-or 14-year-old step-daughter, and has since been convicted of that crime. There is thus ample support in the record for this condition"); *United States v. Mike*, 632 F.3d at 692 ("First, [the conditions] must be reasonably related to at least one of the following: the nature and circumstances of the offense, the defendant's history and characteristics, the deterrence of criminal conduct, the protection of the public from further crimes of the defendant, and the defendant's educational, vocational, medical, or other correction needs. Second they must involve no greater deprivation of liberty that is reasonably necessary to achieve the purpose of deterring criminal activity, protecting the public, and promoting the defendant's rehabilitation. Third, they must be consistent with any pertinent policy statements issued by the Sentencing Commission").

[106] See, e.g., Hamilton, *The "Licentiousness" in Religious Organizations and Why It Is Not Protected Under Religious Liberty Constitutional Provisions*, 18 WILLIAM & MARY BILL OF RIGHTS JOURNAL 953, 969 n.72 (2010); Dubler, *Immoral Purposes: Marriage and the Genus of Illicit Sex*, 115 YALE LAW JOURNAL 756,761 (2005); Friedman, *Name Robbers: Privacy, Blackmail, and Assorted Matters in Legal History*, 30 HOFSTRA LAW REVIEW 1093, 1118 (2002).

[107] 18 U.S.C. 2422(b)("Whoever, using the mail or any facility or means of interstate or foreign commerce, or within the special maritime and territorial jurisdiction of the United States knowingly persuades, induces, entices, or coerces any individual who has not attained the age of 18 years, to engage in prostitution or any sexual activity for which any person can be charged with a criminal offense, or attempts to do so, shall be fined under this title and imprisoned not less than 10 years or for life") (Note that the subsection proscribes the same

conduct when committed within the special maritime and territorial jurisdiction of the United States).

108 *United States v. Berk*, 652 F.3d 132, 138 (1st Cir. 2011), citing in accord *United States v. Cochran*, 534 F.3d 631, 633 (7th Cir. 2008); *United States v. Thomas*, 410 F.3d 1235, 1245 (10th Cir. 2005); *United States v. Brand*, 467 F.3d 179, 201-02 (2d Cir. 2006); and *United States v. Meek*, 366 F.3d 705, 718 (9th Cir. 2004); see also *United States v. Young*, 613 F.3d 735, 742 (8th Cir. 2010).

109 *United States v. Berk*, 652 F.3d 132, 140 (1st Cir. 2011); *United States v. Chambers*, 642 F.3d 588, 592 (7th Cir. 2011); *United States v. Lanzon*, 639 F.3d 1293, 1299 (11th Cir. 2011); *United States v. Hart*, 635 F.3d 850, 855 (6th Cir. 2011); *United States v. Douglas*, 626 F.3d 161, 164 (2d Cir. 2010).

110 *United States v. Berk*, 652 F.3d 132, 140 (1st Cir. 2011); *United States v. Chambers*, 642 F.3d 588, 592 (7th Cir. 2011); *United States v. Lanzon*, 639 F.3d 1293, 1299 (11th Cir. 2011); *United States v. Douglas*, 626 F.3d 161, 164 (2d Cir. 2010); *United States v. Hofus*, 598 F.3d 1171, 1174 (9th Cir. 2010).

111 *United States v. Berk*, 652 F.3d 132, 140 (1st Cir. 2011)("Section 2422(b) criminalizes an intentional attempt to achieve a mental state—a minor's assent—regardless of the accused's intentions vis-a-vis the actual consummation of sexual activities with the minor"); see also *United States v. Berg*, 640 F.3d 239, 252 (7th Cir. 2011), citing in accord *United States v. Lee*, 603 F.3d 904, 914 (11th Cir. 2010); *United States v. Brand*, 467 F.3d 179, 202 (2d Cir. 2006); *United States v. Thomas*, 410 F.3d 1235, 1244 (10th Cir. 2005); and *United States v. Patten*, 397 F.3d 1100, 1103 (8th Cir. 2005).

112 *United States v. Berk*, 652 F.3d 132, 140 (1st Cir. 2011); *United States v. Lanzon*, 639 F.3d 1293, 1299 (11th Cir. 2011); *United States v. Douglas*, 626 F.3d 161, 164 (2d Cir. 2010); *United States v. Nestor*, 574 F.3d 159, 160-62 (3d Cir. 2009).

113 *United States v. Lanzon*, 639 F.3d 1293, 1299 (11th Cir. 2011)("[A]n actual minor victim is not required for an attempt conviction under §2422(b)"); see also, *United States v. Nestor*, 574 F.3d 159, 161 (3d Cir. 2009).

114 *United States v. Brucker*, 646 F.3d 1012, 1018-19 (7th Cir. 2011); *United States v. Hart*, 635 F.3d 850, 858-59 (6th Cir. 2011); *United States v. Farley*, 607 F.3d 1294, 1336-345 (11th Cir. 2010).

115 *United States v. Orr*, 622 F.3d 864, 868-70 (7th Cir. 2010); *United States v. Young*, 613 F.3d 735, 746-48 (8th Cir. 2010); *United States v. Gagliardi*, 506 F.3d 140, 149-50 (2d Cir. 2007).

116 *United States v. Hart*, 635 F.3d 850, 858 (6th Cir. 2011).

117 *United States v. Brucker*, 646 F.3d 1012, 1016-18 (7th Cir. 2011); *United States v. Hughes*, 632 F.3d 956, 960-61 (6th Cir. 2011).

118 *United States v. Hart*, 635 F.3d 850, 856-58 (6th Cir. 2011); *United States v. Farley*, 607 F.3d 1294, 1324 (11th Cir. 2010); *United States v. Gagliardi*, 506 F.3d 140, 149-50 (2d Cir. 2007); *United States v. Gagliardi*, 506 F.3d 140, 145-47 (2d Cir. 2007).

119 *United States v. Brucker*, 646 F.3d 1012, 1016, 1019 (7th Cir. 2011)("For in making the sentencing guidelines advisory [in *Booker*], the Court did not authorize courts to sentence below the minimums proscribed not by the guidelines but by constitutional federal statutes.... We have rejected separation of powers challenges to mandatory minimum sentences, and we see no reason to revisit that holding here"); *United States v. Hughes*, 632 F.3d 956, 961 (6th Cir. 2011); *United States v. Gagliardi*, 506 F.3d 140, 148-49 (2d Cir. 2007).

120 18 U.S.C. 2423(a)("A person who knowingly transports an individual who has not attained the age of 18 years in interstate or foreign commerce, or in any commonwealth, territory or possession of the United States, with intent that the individual engage in prostitution, or in any sexual activity for which any person can be charged with a criminal offense, shall be fined under this title and imprisoned not less than 10 years or for life").

121 18 U.S.C. 2423(e).

[122] 18 U.S.C. 2423(b), (c), and (d), respectively. Attempts or conspiracies to violate any of these are also punishable by imprisonment for not more than 30 years, 18 U.S.C. 2423(e).

[123] *United States v. Broxmeyer*, 616 F.3d 120, 128 (2d Cir. 2010); see also *United States v. Bonty*, 383 F.3d 575, 578 (7th Cir. 2004).

[124] *United States v. Daniels*, 653 F.3d 399, 409-10 (6th Cir. 2011), citing in accord *United States v. Cox*, 577 F.3d 833, 838 (7th Cir. 2009); *United States v. Jones*, 471 F.3d 535, 539 (4th Cir. 2006); *United States v. Griffith*, 284 F.3d 338, 351 (2d Cir. 2002); and *United States v. Taylor*, 239 F.3d 994, 997 (9th Cir. 2001).

[125] *United States v. Hoffman*, 626 F.3d 993, 996 (8th Cir. 2010)("The illicit behavior must be one of the purposes motivating ... the interstate transportation of the minor, but need not be the dominant purpose"); *United States v. Bonty*, 383 F.3d 575, 578 (7th Cir. 2004)("The government need only prove that a significant or compelling purpose the trip— not the dominant purpose—was to commit aggravated assault"); *United States v. Hayward*, 359 F.3d 631, 638 (3d Cir. 2004)("Hayward points to no case in which any Court of Appeals required a jury instruction that criminal sexual activity must be the dominant purpose of interstate travel to support a conviction under 18 U.S.C. §2423(a). The Government relies on decisions by the First, Second, Fifth, Sixth, Seventh, and Tenth Circuits, in which criminal sexual activity was one of a number of multiple motives for interstate travel.... Similarly in this case, the District Court's charge that 'a significant or motivating purpose of the travel across state or foreign boundaries was to have the individual transported engage in illegal sexual activity. In other words, the illegal sexual activity must not have been merely incidental to the trip' was not in error").

[126] 18 U.S.C. 2241(c)("Whoever crosses a State line with intent to engage in a sexual act with a person who has not attained the age of 12 years ... or attempts to do so, shall be fined under this title and imprisoned for not less than 30 years or for life. If the defendant has previously been convicted of another Federal offense under this subsection, or of a State offense that would have been an offense under either such provision had the offense occurred in a Federal prison, unless the death penalty is imposed, the defendant shall be sentenced to life in prison"); e.g., *United States v. King*, 604 F.3d 125, 146 (3d Cir. 2010)(uphold a conviction and 30-year sentence under the travel prong of subsection 2241(c)); *United States v. Farley*, 607 F.3d 1294, 1336-345 (11th Cir. 2010)(reversing a lower court ruling which had held the mandatory minimum sentencing provision of subsection 2241(c) unconstitutionally disproportionate).

[127] 18 U.S.C. 2241(c).

[128] 18 U.S.C. 2241(d)("In a prosecution under subsection (c) of this section, the Government need not prove that the defendant knew that the other person engaging in the sexual act had not attained the age of 12 years").

[129] 18 U.S.C. 1591(a)(1), (a)(2).

[130] 18 U.S.C. 1591(2)("if the offense was not so effected, and the person recruited, enticed, harbored, transported, provided, or obtained had attained the age of 14 years but had not attained the age of 18 years at the time of such offense, by a fine under this title and imprisonment for not less than 10 years or for life").

[131] 18 U.S.C. 1591(b)(1)("[I]f the offense was effected by means of force, threats of force, fraud, or coercion described in subsection (e)(2), or by any combination of such means, or if the person recruited, enticed, harbored, transported, provided, or obtained had not attained the age of 14 years at the time of such offense, by a fine under this title and imprisonment for any term of years not less than 15 or for life").

[132] 18 U.S.C. 1591(a)(1)("Whoever knowingly - (1) in or affecting interstate or foreign commerce, or within the special maritime and territorial jurisdiction of the United States, recruits, entices, harbors, transports, provides, obtains, or maintains by any means a person ... knowing, or in reckless disregard of the fact, that means of force, threats of force, fraud, coercion described in subsection (e)(2), or any combination of such means will be used to cause the person to engage in a commercial sex act, or that the person has not attained the

age of 18 years and will be caused to engage in a commercial sex act, shall be punished as provided in subsection (b).

133 18 U.S.C. 1591(a)(2)("Whoever knowingly ... (2) benefits, financially or by receiving anything of value, from participation in a venture which has engaged in an act described in violation of paragraph (1), knowing, or in reckless disregard of the fact, that means of force, threats of force, fraud, coercion described in subsection (e)(2), or any combination of such means will be used to cause the person to engage in a commercial sex act, or that the person has not attained the age of 18 years and will be caused to engage in a commercial sex act, shall be punished as provided in subsection (b)").

134 *United States v. Todd*, 627 F.3d 329, 333 (9th Cir. 2010); *United States v. Evans*, 476 F.3d 1176, 1178-179 (11th Cir. 2007).

135 *United States v. Anderson*, 560 F.3d 275, 280 (5th Cir. 2009); *United States v. Evans*, 476 F.3d 1176, 1179-180 (11th Cir. 2007).

136 *United States v. Evans*, 476 F.3d 1176, 1180 n.2 (11th Cir. 2007).

137 *United States v. Brooks*, 610 F.3d 1186, 1195 (9th Cir. 2010)("§1591(a) plainly requires proof that the defendant knew that the victim was under the age of eighteen years at the time of crime ...").

138 18 U.S.C. 1591(c)("In a prosecution under subsection (a)(1) in which the defendant had a reasonable opportunity to observe the person so recruited, enticed, harbored, transported, provided, obtained or maintained, the Government need not prove that the defendant knew that the person had not attained the age of 18 years").

139 18 U.S.C. 2245 ("A person who, in the course of an offense under this chapter, or section 1591, 2251, 2251A, 2260,2421, 2422, 2423, or 2425, murders an individual, shall be punished by death or imprisoned for any term of years or for life").

140 18 U.S.C. 1111 (murder within the special maritime and territorial jurisdiction of the United States), 1118 (murder by federal prisoners).

141 18 U.S.C. 2251(e).

142 18 U.S.C. 1593(a)(mandatory restitution); e.g., *United States v. Palmer*, 643 F.3d 1060 (8th Cir. 2011).

143 18 U.S.C. 1593(b)(2)("An order of restitution under this section shall be issued and enforced in accordance with section 3664 in the same manner as an order under section 3663A").

144 18 U.S.C. 1593(c)("As used in this section, the term 'victim' means the individual harmed as a result of a crime under this chapter, including, in the case of a victim who is under 18 years of age, incompetent, incapacitated, or deceased, the legal guardian of the victim or a representative of the victim's estate, or another family member, or any other person appointed as suitable by the court, but in no event shall the defendant be named such representative or guardian").

145 Cf., *United States v. Tsosie*, 639 F.3d 1213, 1220 (9th Cir. 2011).

146 18 U.S.C. 1593(b)(1).

147 18 U.S.C. 1593(b)(3)("As used in this subsection, the term 'full amount of the victim's losses' has the same meaning as provided in section 2259(b)(3) and shall in addition include the greater of the gross income or value to the defendant of the victim's services or labor or the value of the victim's labor as guaranteed under the minimum wage and overtime guarantees of the Fair Labor Standards Act (29 U.S.C. 201 et seq.)"); 18 U.S.C. 2259(b)(3)("For purposes of this subsection, the term 'full amount of the victim's losses' includes any costs incurred by the victim for - (A)medical services relating to physical, psychiatric, or psychological care; (B) physical and occupational therapy or rehabilitation; (C) necessary transportation, temporary housing, and child care expenses; (D) lost income; (E) attorneys' fees, as well as other costs incurred; and (F) any other losses suffered by the victim as a proximate result of the offense").

148 E.g., *United States v. Doe*, 488 F.3d 1154, 1156, 1159-162 (9th Cir. 2007)(ordering restitution under 18 U.S.C. 2259(mandatory restitution in pornography cases) from a defendant

convicted of engaging in sexual conduct with children overseas in violation of 18 U.S.C. 2423(c) and of producing pornography overseas in violation of 18 U.S.C. 2251(c)).

[149] Restitution is mandatory following conviction for a crime of violence, 18 U.S.C. 3663A(a)(1), (c)(1).

[150] 18 U.S.C. 3583(k)("... [T]he authorized term of supervised release for any offense under section 1201 involving a minor victim, and for any offense under section 1591, 2241, 2242, 2243, 2244, 2245, 2250, 2251, 2251A, 2252, 2252A,2260, 2421, 2422, 2423, or 2425, is any term of years not less than 5, or life ...").

[151] 18 U.S.C. 3583(d). The order of supervised release need only include a registration condition when the offender is otherwise required to register, *id.* Federal law requires any defendant convicted of any of the mandatory minimum sex offenses to register, 42 U.S.C. 16913(a), 16911.

[152] 18 U.S.C. 3583(d).

[153] E.g., *United States v. Miller*, 665 F.3d 114, 126 (5th Cir. 2011)("The defendant shall not use any computer at any location, whether or not at his place of employment, residence, or elsewhere, without the prior written permission of the probation officer. The defendant shall not possess or use any phone or any other electronic device that allows access to the internet without prior written permission from the probation officer"); *United States v. Musso*, 643 F.3d 566, (7th Cir. 2011)(The conditions of release require "Musso to ... (3) refrain from frequenting, loitering, or residing within 500 feet of locations where children congregate, (4) have no supervised or unsupervised contact with any minor, and (5) forego volunteer activities that might result in contact with minors").

[154] 18 U.S.C. 2251(e)("Any individual who violates, or attempts or conspires to violate, this section shall be fined under this title and imprisoned not less than 15 years nor more than 30 years, but if such person has one prior conviction under this chapter, section 1591, chapter 71, chapter 109A, or chapter 117, or under section 920 of title 10 (article 120 of the Uniform Code of Military Justice), or under the laws of any State relating to aggravated sexual abuse, sexual abuse, abusive sexual contact involving a minor or ward, or sex trafficking of children, or the production, possession, receipt, mailing, sale, distribution, shipment, or transportation of child pornography, such person shall be fined under this title and imprisoned for not less than 25 years nor more than 50 years, but if such person has 2 or more prior convictions under this chapter, chapter 71, chapter 109A, or chapter 117, or under section 920 of title 10 (article 120 of the Uniform Code of Military Justice), or under the laws of any State relating to the sexual exploitation of children, such person shall be fined under this title and imprisoned not less than 35 years nor more than life. Any organization that violates, or attempts or conspires to violate, this section shall be fined under this title. Whoever, in the course of an offense under this section, engages in conduct that results in the death of a person, shall be punished by death or imprisoned for not less than 30 years or for life").

[155] *Id.*

[156] 18 U.S.C. 2256(1).

[157] 18 U.S.C. 2251(a), (b), (c), (d).

[158] *United States v. Fletcher*, 634 F.3d 395, 400-405 (7th Cir. 2011); *United States v. Heath*, 624 F.3d 884, 886 (8th Cir. 2010); *United States v. Humphrey*, 608 F.3d 955, 957-62 (6th Cir. 2010); *United States v. Malloy*, 568 F.3d 166, 171 (4th Cir. 2009); *United States v. Griffith*, 284 F.3d 338, 349 (2d Cir. 2002); but see *United States v. United States District Court*, 858 F.2d 534, 543 (9th Cir. 1988)("A defendant may avoid conviction only showing, by clear and convincing evidence, that he did not know, and could not reasonable have learned, that the actor or actress was under 18 years of age").

[159] 18 U.S.C. 2256(5) 'visual depiction' includes undeveloped film and videotape, data stored on computer disk or by electronic means which is capable of conversion into a visual image, and data which is capable of conversion into a visual image that has been transmitted by any means, whether or not stored in a permanent format").

[160] 18 U.SC. 2256(2)(A)("Except as provided in subparagraph (B), 'sexually explicit conduct' means actual or simulated - (i) sexual intercourse, including genital-genital, oral-genital, anal-genital, or oral-anal, whether between persons of the same or opposite sex; (ii) bestiality; (iii) masturbation; (iv) sadistic or masochistic abuse; or (v) lascivious exhibition of the genitals or pubic area of any person").

[161] *United States v. Johnson*, 639 F.3d 433, 439-40 (8th Cir. 2011)("In determining whether images are "lascivious," we have referred to the criteria listed in *United States v. Dost*, 636 F.Supp. 828, 832 (S.D. Cal. 1986), aff'd sub nom., *United States v. Wiegand*, 812 F.2d 1239 (9th Cir. 1987). The factors in *Dost* included (1) whether the focal point of the picture is on the minor's genitals or pubic area; (2) whether the setting of the picture is sexually suggestive; (3) whether the minor is depicted in unnatural poses or inappropriate attire considering the minor's age; (4) whether the minor is fully or partially clothed or is nude; (5) whether the picture suggests sexual coyness or a willingness to engage in sexual activity; and (6) whether the image is intended to elicit a sexual response in the viewer.... However, while we consider these criteria, they are 'neither definitive nor exhaustive"); see also *United States v. Steen*, 634 F.3d 822, 826-27 (5th Cir. 2011); *United States v. Brown*, 579 F.3d 672, 680-83 (6th Cir. 2009); *United States v. Overton*, 573 F.3d 679, 686-90 (9th Cir. 2009); *United States v. Rivera*, 546 F.3d 245, 250 (2d Cir. 2008); *United States v. Frabizio,* 459 F.3d 80, 87 (1st Cir. 2006).

[162] 18 U.S.C. 2251("(a) Any person who employs, uses, persuades, induces, entices, or coerces any minor to engage in, or who has a minor assist any other person to engage in ... with the intent that such minor engage in, any sexually explicit conduct for the purpose of producing any visual depiction of such conduct or for the purpose of transmitting a live visual depiction of such conduct, shall be punished as provided under subsection (e), if such person knows or has reason to know that such visual depiction will be transported or transmitted using any means or facility of interstate or foreign commerce.... (e) Any individual who violates, or attempts or conspires to violate, this section shall...."); see, e.g., *United States v. Coutentos*, 651 F.3d 809, 823 (8th Cir. 2011)("To convict Coutentos of producing child pornography under 18 U.S.C. §2251(a) and (d)(2000), the government must have established that (1) at a time when K.C. or S.Z., or both, were under eighteen years of age; (2) Coutentos used, persuaded, or induced K.C. or S.Z., or both, to engage in sexually explicit conduct; (3) Coutentos voluntarily and intentionally did this for the purpose of producing at least one visual depiction of such conduct; and (4) at least one those depictions was produced using a camera that had been shipped and transported in interstate or foreign commerce. See §2251(a). The elements are the same to prove attempted sexual exploitation of a minor except that the attempt charge requires only that Coutentos attempted to produce a visual depiction and that he carried out some act which was a substantial step toward that production. See §2251").

[163] 18 U.S.C. 2251(a)("Any person who employs, uses, persuades, induces, entices, or coerces any minor to engage in, or who has a minor assist any other person to engage in, or who transports any minor in or affecting interstate or foreign commerce, or in any Territory or Possession of the United States, with the intent that such minor engage in, any sexually explicit conduct for the purpose of producing any visual depiction of such conduct or for the purpose of transmitting a live visual depiction of such conduct, shall be punished as provided under subsection (e), if such person knows or has reason to know that such visual depiction will be transported or transmitted using any means or facility of interstate or foreign commerce or in or affecting interstate or foreign commerce or mailed, if that visual depiction was produced or transmitted using materials that have been mailed, shipped, or transported in or affecting interstate or foreign commerce by any means, including by computer, or if such visual depiction has actually been transported or transmitted using any means or facility of interstate or foreign commerce or in or affecting interstate or foreign commerce or mailed").

[164] *United States v. Culver*, 598 F.3d 740, 746-47 (11th Cir. 2010); *United States v. McCloud*, 590 F.3d 560, 568 (8th Cir. 2009); *United States v. Malloy*, 568 F.3d 166, 179-80 (4th Cir. 2009).

[165] *United States v. Malloy*, 568 F.3d 166, 180 (4th Cir. 2009); *United States v. Rivera*, 546 F.3d 245, 254-55 (2d Cir.2008); *United States v. Polk*, 546 F.3d 74, 74-8 (1st Cir. 2008); *United States v. Paton*, 535 F.3d 829, 837-38 (8th Cir. 2008).

[166] 18 U.S.C. 2251(b)("Any parent, legal guardian, or person having custody or control of a minor who knowingly permits such minor to engage in, or to assist any other person to engage in, sexually explicit conduct for the purpose of producing any visual depiction of such conduct or for the purpose of transmitting a live visual depiction of such conduct shall be punished as provided under subsection (e) of this section, if such parent, legal guardian, or person knows or has reason to know that such visual depiction will be transported or transmitted using any means or facility of interstate or foreign commerce or in or affecting interstate or foreign commerce or mailed, if that visual depiction was produced or transmitted using materials that have been mailed, shipped, or transported in or affecting interstate or foreign commerce by any means, including by computer, or if such visual depiction has actually been transported or transmitted using any means or facility of interstate or foreign commerce or in or affecting interstate or foreign commerce or mailed"); see, e.g., *United States v. O'Connor*, 650 F.3d 839, 857-58 (2d Cir. 2011); *United States v. Paige*, 604 F.3d 1268, 1270 (11th Cir. 2010).

[167] Section 2251A is discussed in a later section of this report.

[168] 18 U.S.C. 2251(c)("(1) Any person who, in a circumstance described in paragraph (2), employs, uses, persuades, induces, entices, or coerces any minor to engage in, or who has a minor assist any other person to engage in, any sexually explicit conduct outside of the United States, its territories or possessions, for the purpose of producing any visual depiction of such conduct, shall be punished as provided under subsection (e). (2) The circumstance referred to in paragraph (1) is that - (A) the person intends such visual depiction to be transported to the United States, its territories or possessions, by any means, including by using any means or facility of interstate or foreign commerce or mail; or (B) the person transports such visual depiction to the United States, its territories or possessions, by any means, including by using any means or facility of interstate or foreign commerce or mail"); see, e.g., United States v. Deverso, 518 F.3d 1250, 1257 (11th Cir. 2008).

[169] *United States v. Rowe*, 414 F.3d 271, 278 (2d Cir. 2005).

[170] 18 U.S.C. 2251(d)("(1) Any person who, in a circumstance described in paragraph (2), knowingly makes, prints, or publishes, or causes to be made, printed, or published, any notice or advertisement seeking or offering - (A) to receive, exchange, buy, produce, display, distribute, or reproduce, any visual depiction, if the production of such visual depiction involves the use of a minor engaging in sexually explicit conduct and such visual depiction is of such conduct; or (B) participation in any act of sexually explicit conduct by or with any minor for the purpose of producing a visual depiction of such conduct; shall be punished as provided under subsection (e)").

[171] 18 U.S.C. 2251(d)("... (2) The circumstance referred to in paragraph (1) is that - (A) such person knows or has reason to know that such notice or advertisement will be transported using any means or facility of interstate or foreign commerce or in or affecting interstate or foreign commerce by any means including by computer or mailed; or (B) such notice or advertisement is transported using any means or facility of interstate or foreign commerce or in or affecting interstate or foreign commerce by any means including by computer or mailed").

[172] *United States v. Rowe*, 414 F.3d 271, 277 (2d Cir. 2005).

[173] 18 U.S.C. 2251A(a)("Any parent, legal guardian, or other person having custody or control of a minor who sells or otherwise transfers custody or control of such minor, or offers to sell or otherwise transfer custody of such minor either - (1) with knowledge that, as a consequence of the sale or transfer, the minor will be portrayed in a visual depiction engaging in, or assisting another person to engage in, sexually explicit conduct; or (2) with intent to

promote either (A) the engaging in of sexually explicit conduct by such minor for the purpose of producing any visual depiction of such conduct; or (B) the rendering of assistance by the minor to any other person to engage in sexually explicit conduct for the purpose of producing any visual depiction of such conduct; shall be punished by imprisonment for not less than 30 years or for life and by a fine under this title, if any of the circumstances described in subsection (c) of this section exist"). Subsection 2251A(b) contains similar provisions and penalties relating to those who acquire or seek to acquire custody or control of a child for purposes of producing child pornography.

[174] 18 U.S.C. 2256(7).

[175] *United States v. Block*, 635 F.3d 721, 723 (5th Cir. 2011).

[176] *United States v. Buculei*, 262 F.3d 322, 331 (4th Cir. 2001).

[177] *United States v. Frank*, 599 F.3d 1221, 1234 (11th Cir. 2010)("Frank argues that there was insufficient evidence that he 'purchas[ed] ... a minor,' as required by 18 U.S.C. §2241A(b), because (1) the term 'purchase' requires that a defendant purchase a minor from a third party, rather than from the minor herself; and (2) the phrase 'purchase[] or otherwise obtain[] custody or control' requires that purchase must be a form of control, which Frank argues is only achieved through 'sexual slavery,' such as forced prostitution or captivity for the purpose of producing child pornography. We disagree").

[178] 18 U.S.C. 2251A(c)("the circumstances referred to in subsections (a) and (b) are that - (1) in the course of the conduct described in such subsections the minor or the actor traveled in or was transported in or affecting interstate or foreign commerce; (2) any offer described in such subsections was communicated or transported using any means or facility of interstate or foreign commerce or in or affecting interstate or foreign commerce by any means including by computer or mail; or (3) the conduct described in such subsections took place in any territory or possession of the United States").

[179] 18 U.S.C. 2252(a)(1), (2), (3). 18 U.S.C. 2252(b)(1)("Whoever violates, or attempts or conspires to violate, paragraph (1), (2), or (3) of subsection (a) shall be fined under this title and imprisoned not less than 5 years and not more than 20 years, but if such person has a prior conviction under this chapter, section 1591, chapter 71, chapter 109A, or chapter 117, or under section 920 of title 10 (article 120 of the Uniform Code of Military Justice), or under the laws of any State relating to aggravated sexual abuse, sexual abuse, or abusive sexual conduct involving a minor or ward, or the production, possession, receipt, mailing, sale, distribution, shipment, or transportation of child pornography, or sex trafficking of children, such person shall be fined under this title and imprisoned for not less than15 years nor more than 40 years").

[180] *Id.*

[181] 18 U.S.C. 2252(a)(4), (b)(2).

[182] 18 U.S.C. 2252(b)(1). 18 U.S.C. 2252(b)(2)("Whoever violates, or attempts or conspires to violate, paragraph (4) of subsection (a) shall be fined under this title or imprisoned not more than 10 years, or both, but if such person has a prior conviction under this chapter, chapter 71, chapter 109A, or chapter 117, or under section 920 of title 10 (article 120 of the Uniform Code of Military Justice), or under the laws of any State relating to aggravated sexual abuse, sexual abuse, or abusive sexual conduct involving a minor or ward, or the production, possession, receipt, mailing, sale, distribution, shipment, or transportation of child pornography, such person shall be fined under this title and imprisoned for not less than 10 years nor more than 20 years").

[183] 18 U.S.C. 2252(a)("Any person who - (1) knowingly transports or ships using any means or facility of interstate or foreign commerce or in or affecting interstate or foreign commerce by any means including by computer or mails, any visual depiction, if - (A) the producing of such visual depiction involves the use of a minor engaging in sexually explicit conduct; and (B) such visual depiction is of such conduct ... shall be punished as provided in subsection (b) of this section").

[184] 18 U.S.C. 2252(b)(1).

[185] *United States v. Chambers*, 441 F.3d 438, 449 (6th Cir. 2006).
[186] *United States v. Sims*, 428 F.3d 945, 957 (10th Cir. 2005).
[187] *United States v. X-Citment Video, Inc*., 513 U.S. 64, 78 (1994).
[188] *United States v. Lewis*, 605 F.3d 395, 403 (6th Cir. 2010).
[189] *United States v. Polanco*, 451 F.3d 308, 310 (3d Cir. 2006).
[190] *United States v. Chambers*, 441 F.3d 438, 450 (6th Cir. 2006).
[191] *United States v. Osborne*, 551 F.3d 718, 721 (7th Cir. 2009).
[192] 18 U.S.C. 2252(a)("Any person who ... (2) knowingly receives, or distributes, any visual depiction using any means or facility of interstate or foreign commerce or that has been mailed, or has been shipped or transported in or affecting interstate or foreign commerce, or which contains materials which have been mailed or so shipped or transported, by any means including by computer, or knowingly reproduces any visual depiction for distribution using any means or facility of interstate or foreign commerce or in or affecting interstate or foreign commerce or through the mails, if - (A) the producing of such visual depiction involves the use of a minor engaging in sexually explicit conduct; and (B) such visual depiction is of such conduct ... shall be punished as provided in subsection (b) of this section"); 18 U.S.C. 2252(b)(1).
[193] *United States v. Schwarte*, 645 F.3d 1022, 1032 (8th Cir. 2011). After the events in *Schwarte* occurred, Congress expanded the subsection's jurisdictional reach by adding transportation and transmissions "affecting interstate or foreign commerce," P.L. 110-358, 103(b), 122 Stat. 4003 (2008).
[194] *United States v. Winkler*, 639 F.3d 692, 696 (5th Cir. 2011), citing inter alia, *United States v. Dobbs*, 629 F.3d 1199, 1201, 1207 (10th Cir. 2011)(emphasis in the original)("[T]he lack of a search-and-creation pattern ... when combined with the absence of any evidence establishing that the defendant ever saw the images, forefends any view that *knowing* receipt could have been found by the jury"); *United States v. Kuchinski*, 469 F.3d 853, 861-62 (9th Cir. 2006)"Citing the fact that there was no evidence the defendant was a sophisticated computer user, that he tried to get access to the cache files, or that he knew of the cache's existence"); *United States v. Bass*, 411 F.3d 1198 (10th Cir. 2005)("In *Bass*, the court relied on the fact that the defendant used software specifically aimed at eliminating the digital residue of his illicit activities to determine that the defendant did knowingly receive the files stored in his internet cache").
[195] E.g., *United States v. Winkler*, 639 F.3d 692, 699 (5th Cir. 2011)("Those facts speak to a pattern of child pornography receipt and possession that could also have caused a rational jury to conclude that Winkler knowing received the files in Count One. In sum, this is not the exceptional case in which the government has persisted in bringing a criminal prosecution against the unknowing victim of a computer's inner workings").
[196] *United States v. Szymanski*, 631 F.3d 794, 798-99 (6th Cir. 2011); *United States v. Pires*, 642 F.3d 1, 8 (1st Cir. 2011); *United States v. McNealy*, 625 F.3d 858, 870 (5th Cir. 2010), all citing *United States v. X-Citement Video, Inc*., 513 U.S. 64, 70-3 (1994).
[197] *United States v. Pires,* 642 F.3d 1, 9 (1st Cir. 2011); see also, *United States v. MacEwan*, 445 F.3d 237, 244 (3d Cir. 2006)("[B]ecause of the very interstate nature of the Internet, once a user submits a connection request to a website server or an image is transmitted from the website server back to the user the data has traveled in interstate commerce").
[198] *United States v. Pires,* 642 F.3d 1, 8 (1st Cir. 2011)(internal citations omitted)("To prove attempt, the government must show both that the accused intended to commit the underlying substantive offense (here, knowing receipt of child pornography) and that he took a substantial step toward committing that crime. But this does not mean that the government bore a burden to prove each element of the underlying offense. While the underlying offense in this case requires the receipt of images of real-life minors engaged in sexually explicit conduct, the government in an attempt case has no burden to prove that the appellant knew that the downloaded file actually contained such images. Rather, the

government is required to prove that the appellant believed that the received file contained such images"); *United States v. Dobbs*, 629 F.3d 1199, 1208-209 (10th Cir. 2011).

199 *United States v. Linngren*, 652 F.3d 868, 870-71 (8th Cir. 2011); United States v. Becker, 625 F.3d 1309, 1310-313 (10th Cir. 2010)

200 18 U.S.C. 2252(a)(3), (b)(1).

201 18 U.S.C. 2252(b)(1).

202 18 U.S.C. 2252(a)(3)("Any person who ... (A) in the special maritime and territorial jurisdiction of the United States, or on any land or building owned by, leased to, or otherwise used by or under the control of the Government of the United States, or in the Indian country as defined in section 1151 of this title, knowingly sells or possesses with intent to sell any visual depiction ... shall be punished as provided in subsection (b) of this section").

203 18 U.S.C. 2252(a)(3)("Any person who ... (B) knowingly sells or possesses with intent to sell any visual depiction that has been mailed, shipped, or transported using any means or facility of interstate or foreign commerce, or has been shipped or transported in or affecting interstate or foreign commerce, or which was produced using materials which have been mailed or so shipped or transported using any means or facility of interstate or foreign commerce, including by computer, if - (i) the producing of such visual depiction involves the use of a minor engaging in sexually explicit conduct; and (ii) such visual depiction is of such conduct ... shall be punished as provided in subsection (b) of this section").

204 18 U.S.C. 2252(b)(2).

205 18 U.S.C. 2252(a)(4)("Any person who ... either (A) in the special maritime and territorial jurisdiction of the United States, or on any land or building owned by, leased to, or otherwise used by or under the control of the Government of the United States, or in the Indian country as defined in section 1151 of this title, knowingly possesses, or knowingly accesses with intent to view, 1 or more books, magazines, periodicals, films, video tapes, or other matter which contain any visual depiction; or (B) knowingly possesses, or knowingly accesses with intent to view, 1 or more books, magazines, periodicals, films, video tapes, or other matter which contain any visual depiction that has been mailed, or has been shipped or transported using any means or facility of interstate or foreign commerce or in or affecting interstate or foreign commerce, or which was produced using materials which have been mailed or so shipped or transported, by any means including by computer, if - (i) the producing of such visual depiction involves the use of a minor engaging in sexually explicit conduct; and (ii) such visual depiction is of such conduct; shall be punished as provided in subsection (b) of this section").

206 18 U.S.C. 2252(b)(2); *United States v. Stults*, 575 F.3d 834, 844-45 (9th Cir. 2009); *United States v. McCutchen*, 419 F.3d 1122, 1125 (10th Cir. 2005).

207 *United States v. Stults*, 575 F.3d 834, 846 (9th Cir. 2009); *United States v. McCutchen*, 419 F.3d 1122, 1125 (10th Cir. 2005); cf., *United States v. Rezin*, 322 F.3d 443, 447-48 (7th Cir. 2003).

208 *United States v. Stults*, 575 F.3d 834, 845 (9th Cir. 2009).

209 *Id.*

210 18 U.S.C. 2252(b).

211 18 U.S.C. 2252(c)("It shall be an affirmative defense to a charge of violating paragraph (4) of subsection (a) that the defendant - (1) possessed less than three matters containing any visual depiction proscribed by that paragraph; and (2) promptly and in good faith, and without retaining or allowing any person, other than a law enforcement agency, to access any visual depiction or copy thereof - (A) took reasonable steps to destroy each such visual depiction; or (B) reported the matter to a law enforcement agency and afforded that agency access to each such visual depiction").

212 Compare 18 U.S.C. 2252 (1994 ed. & Supp. II), with 18 U.S.C. 2252A (1994 ed. Supp. II); see also, U.S. Department of Justice, *Criminal Resource Manual* §1969 (2000)("Title 18

U.S.C. §2252A is identical to 18 U.S.C. §2252....”), available at http://www.justice.gov/usao/eousa/foia_reading_room/usam/title9/crm01969.htm.

[213] Then, as now, the prohibitions of subsection 2252A(a) reached “any visual depiction, including any photograph, film, video, picture, or computer or computer-generated image or picture, whether made or produced by electronic, mechanical, or other means, of sexually explicit conduct, where - (A) the production of such visual depiction involves the use of a minor engaging in sexually explicit conduct; (B) such visual depiction is a digital image, computer image, or computer-generated image that is, or is indistinguishable from, that of a minor engaging in sexually explicit conduct; or (C) such visual depiction has been created, adapted, or modified to appear that an identifiable minor is engaging in sexually explicit conduct,” 18 U.S.C. 2256(8). The Supreme Court in *Ashcroft v. Free Speech Coalition*, 535 U.S. 234, 256 (2002) found an earlier version of paragraph 2256(8)(B)(“appears to be a minor”) overbroad and impermissible under the First Amendment. It found the language in then paragraph 2256(8)(D)(“conveys the impression”) overbroad as well, *id.* at 258. Congress subsequently amended paragraph 2256(8)(B) and repealed paragraph 2256(8)(D), P.L. 108-21, §§502(a)(1), 502(a)(3), 117 Stat. 678 (2003).

[214] 18 U.S.C. 2252A(b)(1).

[215] 18 U.S.C. 2252A(b)(1), (b)(2).

[216] 18 U.S.C. 2252A(g)(“(1) Whoever engages in a child exploitation enterprise shall be fined under this title and imprisoned for any term of years not less than 20 or for life. (2) A person engages in a child exploitation enterprise for the purposes of this section if the person violates section 1591, section 1201 if the victim is a minor, or chapter 109A (involving a minor victim), 110 (except for sections 2257 and 2257A), or 117 (involving a minor victim), as a part of a series of felony violations constituting three or more separate incidents and involving more than one victim, and commits those offenses in concert with three or more other persons”).

[217] 18 U.S.C. 2252A(a)(1), (b)(1).

[218] 18 U.S.C. 2252A(b)(1)(“Whoever violates, or attempts or conspires to violate, paragraph (1), (2), (3), (4), or (6) of subsection (a) shall be fined under this title and imprisoned not less than 5 years and not more than 20 years, but, if such person has a prior conviction under this chapter, section 1591, chapter 71, chapter 109A, or chapter 117, or under section 920 of title 10 (article 120 of the Uniform Code of Military Justice), or under the laws of any State relating to aggravated sexual abuse, sexual abuse, or abusive sexual conduct involving a minor or ward, or the production, possession, receipt, mailing, sale, distribution, shipment, or transportation of child pornography, or sex trafficking of children, such person shall be fined under this title and imprisoned for not less than 15 years nor more than 40 years”).

[219] *United States v. Wright*, 625 F.3d 583, 590-601 (9th Cir. 2010).

[220] *United States v. Tenuto*, 593 F.3d 695, 698-99 (7th Cir. 2010).

[221] 18 U.S.C. 2252A(c).

[222] 18 U.S.C. 2252A(c)(“It shall be an affirmative defense to a charge of violating paragraph (1), (2), (3)(A), (4), or (5) of subsection (a) that - (1)(A) the alleged child pornography was produced using an actual person or persons engaging in sexually explicit conduct; and (B) each such person was an adult at the time the material was produced; or (2) the alleged child pornography was not produced using any actual minor or minors.

“No affirmative defense under subsection (c)(2) shall be available in any prosecution that involves child pornography as described in section 2256(8)(C). A defendant may not assert an affirmative defense to a charge of violating paragraph (1), (2), (3)(A), (4), or (5) of subsection (a) unless, within the time provided for filing pretrial motions or at such time prior to trial as the judge may direct, but in no event later than 14 days before the commencement of the trial, the defendant provides the court and the United States with notice of the intent to assert such defense and the substance of any expert or other specialized testimony or evidence upon which the defendant intends to rely. If the defendant fails to comply with this subsection, the court shall, absent a finding of extraordinary circumstances that prevented timely compliance, prohibit the defendant from asserting such defense to a charge of violating paragraph (1), (2), (3)(A), (4), or (5) of subsection (a) or presenting any evidence for which the defendant has failed to provide proper and timely notice").

18 U.S.C. 2256(8)(C)(" 'child pornography' means any visual depiction, including any photograph, film, video, picture, or computer or computer-generated image or picture, whether made or produced by electronic, mechanical, or other means, of sexually explicit conduct, where ... (C) such visual depiction has been created, adapted, or modified to appear that an identifiable minor is engaging in sexually explicit conduct").

[223] 18 U.S.C. 2252A("(a) Any person who ... (2) knowingly receives or distributes—(A) any child pornography that has been mailed, or using any means or facility of interstate or foreign commerce shipped or transported in or affecting interstate or foreign commerce by any means, including by computer; or (B) any material that contains child pornography that has been mailed, or using any means or facility of interstate or foreign commerce shipped or transported in or affecting interstate or foreign commerce by any means, including by computer ... shall be punished as provided in subsection (b). (b)(1) Whoever violates, or attempts or conspires to violate paragraph ... (2) ... shall be ... imprisoned not less than 5 years ...").

[224] *Id.*

[225] 18 U.S.C. 2252A(b)(1)("Whoever violates, or attempts or conspires to violate, paragraph (1), (2), (3), (4), or (6) of subsection (a) shall be fined under this title and imprisoned not less than 5 years and not more than 20 years, but, if such person has a prior conviction under this chapter, section 1591, chapter 71, chapter 109A, or chapter 117, or under section 920 of title 10 (article 120 of the Uniform Code of Military Justice), or under the laws of any State relating to aggravated sexual abuse, sexual abuse, or abusive sexual conduct involving a minor or ward, or the production, possession, receipt, mailing, sale, distribution, shipment, or transportation of child pornography, or sex trafficking of children, such person shall be fined under this title and imprisoned for not less than 15 years nor more than 40 years").

[226] *United States v. Pruitt*, 638 F.3d 763, 766 (11th Cir. 2011).

[227] *Id.*

[228] *United States v. Bauer*, 626 F.3d 1004, 1007-1008 (8th Cir. 2010).

[229] *Id.*

[230] *United States v. Dudeck*, 657 F.3d 424, 428-29 (6th Cir. 2011), citing in accord *United States v. Muhlenbruch*, 634 F.3d 987, 1003-04 (8th Cir. 2011); *United States v. Bobb*, 577 F.3d 1366, 1373-375 (11th Cir. 2009); *United States v. Miller*, 527 F.3d 54,72 (3d Cir. 2008).

[231] *United States v. Ehle*, 640 F.3d 689, 694-95 (6th Cir. 2011); *United States v. Overton*, 573 F.3d 679, 695 (9th Cir. 2009).

[232] *United States v. Dudeck*, 657 F.3d 424, 430 (6th Cir. 2011)("[W]hile possession of child pornography is generally a lesser-included offense of receipt of child pornography, conviction under both statutes is permissible if separate conduct is found to underlie the two offenses"); *United States v. Bobb*, 577 F.3d 1366, 1375 (11th Cir. 2009); *United States v. Overton*, 573 F.3d 679, 695 (9th Cir. 2009).

[233] *United States v. Dudeck*, 657 F.3d 424, 431 (6th Cir. 2011),

[234] 18 U.S.C. 2252A("(a) Any person who ... (3) knowingly - (A) reproduces any child pornography for distribution through the mails, or using any means or facility of interstate or foreign commerce or in or affecting interstate or foreign commerce by any means, including by computer; or (B) advertises, promotes, presents, distributes, or solicits through the mails, or using any means or facility of interstate or foreign commerce or in or affecting interstate or foreign commerce by any means, including by computer, any material or purported material in a manner that reflects the belief, or that is intended to cause another to believe, that the material or purported material is, or contains - (i) an obscene visual depiction of a minor engaging in sexually explicit conduct; or (ii) a visual depiction of an

actual minor engaging in sexually explicit conduct ... shall be punished as provided in subsection (b)"); 18 U.S.C. 2252A(b)(1).

[235] 18 U.S.C. 2252A(a)(3)(A), (a)(3)(B).

[236] *United States v. Williams*, 553 U.S. 285, 292-307 (2008).

[237] *Id.* at 294.

[238] *Id.* at 295.

[239] *Id.*

[240] *Id.* at 296.

[241] *Id.*

[242] 18 U.S.C. 2252A(c)(emphasis added)("It shall be an affirmative defense to a charge of violating paragraph (1), (2),*(3)(A)*, (4), or (5) of subsection (a) that - (1)(A) the alleged child pornography was produced using an actual person or persons engaging in sexually explicit conduct; and (B) each such person was an adult at the time the material was produced; or (2) the alleged child pornography was not produced using any actual minor or minors").

[243] 18 U.S.C. 2252A(a)(4), (b)(1).

[244] 18 U.S.C. 2252A("(a) Any person who ... (4) ... (A) in the special maritime and territorial jurisdiction of the United States, or on any land or building owned by, leased to, or otherwise used by or under the control of the United States Government, or in the Indian country (as defined in section 1151), knowingly sells or possesses with the intent to sell any child pornography ... shall be punished as provided in subsection (b)").

[245] 18 U.S.C. 2252A("(a) Any person who ... (4) ... (B) knowingly sells or possesses with the intent to sell any child pornography that has been mailed, or shipped or transported using any means or facility of interstate or foreign commerce or in or affecting interstate or foreign commerce by any means, including by computer, or that was produced using materials that have been mailed, or shipped or transported in or affecting interstate or foreign commerce by any means, including by computer ... shall be punished as provided in subsection (b)").

[246] 18 U.S.C. 2252A(c).

[247] 18 U.S.C. 2252A("(a) Any person who ... (6) knowingly distributes, offers, sends, or provides to a minor any visual depiction, including any photograph, film, video, picture, or computer generated image or picture, whether made or produced by electronic, mechanical, or other means, where such visual depiction is, or appears to be, of a minor engaging in sexually explicit conduct ... for purposes of inducing or persuading a minor to participate in any activity that is illegal ... shall be punished as provided in subsection (b)"); 18 U.S.C. 2252A(b)(1).

[248] 18 U.S.C. 2252A(b)(1).

[249] 18 U.S.C. 2252A("(a) Any person who ... (6) knowingly ... offers ... to a minor any visual depiction ... where such visual depiction is, or appears to be, of a minor engaging in sexually explicit conduct - (A) that has been mailed, shipped, or transported using any means or facility of interstate or foreign commerce or in or affecting interstate or foreign commerce by any means, including by computer; (B) that was produced using materials that have been mailed, shipped, or transported in or affecting interstate or foreign commerce by any means, including by computer; or (C) which distribution, offer, sending, or provision is accomplished using the mails or any means or facility of interstate or foreign commerce, for purposes of inducing or persuading a minor to participate in any activity that is illegal ... shall be punished as provided in subsection (b)").

[250] 18 U.S.C. 2252A(c)("It shall be an affirmative defense to a charger of violating paragraph (a), (2), (3)(A), (4), or (5) of subsection (a) that ...").

[251] 18 U.S.C. 2252A(a)(5), (b)(1).

[252] 18 U.S.C. 2252A(b)("... (2) Whoever violates, or attempts or conspires to violate, subsection (a)(5) shall be fined under this title or imprisoned not more than 10 years, or both, but, if such person has a prior conviction under this chapter, chapter 71, chapter 109A, or chapter 117, or under section 920 of title 10 (article 120 of the Uniform Code of Military Justice),

or under the laws of any State relating to aggravated sexual abuse, sexual abuse, or abusive sexual conduct involving a minor or ward, or the production, possession, receipt, mailing, sale, distribution, shipment, or transportation of child pornography, such person shall be fined under this title and imprisoned for not less than 10 years nor more than 20 years").

[253] 18 U.S.C. 2252A("(a) Any person who ... (5) ... (A) in the special maritime and territorial jurisdiction of the United States, or on any land or building owned by, leased to, or otherwise used by or under the control of the United States Government, or in the Indian country (as defined in section 1151), knowingly possesses, or knowingly accesses with intent to view, any book, magazine, periodical, film, videotape, computer disk, or any other material that contains an image of child pornography ... shall be punished as provided in subsection (b)").

[254] 18 U.S.C. 2252A("(a) Any person who ... (5) ... (B) knowingly possesses, or knowingly accesses with intent to view, any book, magazine, periodical, film, videotape, computer disk, or any other material that contains an image of child pornography that has been mailed, or shipped or transported using any means or facility of interstate or foreign commerce or in or affecting interstate or foreign commerce by any means, including by computer, or that was produced using materials that have been mailed, or shipped or transported in or affecting interstate or foreign commerce by any means, including by computer ... shall be punished as provided in subsection (b)").

[255] 18 U.S.C. 2252A(c)("It shall be an affirmative defense to a charge of violating paragraph ... (5) of subsection (a) that - (1)(A) the alleged child pornography was produced using an actual person or persons engaging in sexually explicit conduct; and (B) each such person was an adult at the time the material was produced; or (2) the alleged child pornography was not produced using any actual minor or minors").

[256] 18 U.S.C. 2252A(g)(1).

[257] 18 U.S.C. 2252A(g)(2); see also *United States v. Daniels*, 653 F.3d 399, 411 (6th Cir. 2011)("The statute thus requires that the government prove: (1) the defendant committed at least three separate predicate offenses; (2) more than one underage victim was involved; and (3) at least three other persons acted 'in concert' with the defendant to commit the predicate offenses").

[258] *United States v. Daniels*, 653 F.3d 399, 412 (6th Cir. 2011).

[259] *United States v. Wayerski*, 624 F.3d 1342, 1351 (11th Cir. 2010)("Because the defendants' conspiracy convictions did not require proof of facts different from the child exploitation enterprise offense's in concert requirement, we hold that the defendants' conspiracy convictions were lesser included offenses and violated the Double Jeopardy Clause"). The Court held, however, that subsection 2252A(g) was not unconstitutional vague as applied to the defendants, *id.* at 1349.

[260] 18 U.S.C. 2259 (mandatory restitution); e.g., *United States v. Doe*, 488 F.3d 1154 (9th Cir. 2007).

[261] 18 U.S.C. 2259(b)(2)("An order of restitution under this section shall be issued and enforced in accordance with section 3664 in the same manner as an order under section 3663A").

[262] 18 U.S.C. 2259(c)("As used in this section, the term 'victim' means the individual harmed as a result of a crime under this chapter, including, in the case of a victim who is under 18 years of age, incompetent, incapacitated, or deceased, the legal guardian of the victim or a representative of the victim's estate, or another family member, or any other person appointed as suitable by the court, but in no event shall the defendant be named such representative or guardian"); cf., *United States v. Tsosie*, 639 F.3d 1213, 1220 (9th Cir. 2011).

[263] 18 U.S.C. 2259(b)(3)("For purposes of this subsection, the term 'full amount of the victim's losses' includes any costs incurred by the victim for - (A) medical services relating to physical, psychiatric, or psychological care; (B) physical and occupational therapy or rehabilitation; (C) necessary transportation, temporary housing, and child care expenses;

(D) lost income; (E) attorneys' fees, as well as other costs incurred; and (F) any other losses suffered by the victim as a proximate result of the offense").

[264] 18 U.S.C. 3583(k)("... [T]he authorized term of supervised release for any offense under section 1201 involving a minor victim, and for any offense under section 1591, 2241, 2242, 2243, 2244, 2245, 2250, 2251, 2251A, 2252, 2252A,2260, 2421, 2422, 2423, or 2425, is any term of years not less than 5, or life ...").

[265] 18 U.S.C. 3583(d). The order of supervised release need only include a registration condition when the offender is otherwise required to register, *id*. Federal law requires any defendant convicted of any of the mandatory minimum sex offenses to register, 42 U.S.C. 16913(a), 16911.

[266] E.g., *United States v. Demers*, 634 F.3d 982, 983 (8th Cir. 2011)(A condition of supervised release denied the defendant "access [to] the Internet from any location without prior approval by the probation office and for a justified reason"); *United States v. Angle*, 598 F.3d 352, 360 (7th Cir. 2010)("[T]he district court imposed as a special condition of supervised release that Angle 'shall not have personal access to computer Internet services'").

[267] 18 U.S.C. 3583(d); *United States v. Thompson*, 653 F.3d 688, 691 (8th Cir. 2011); *United States v. Albertson*, 645 F.3d 191, 196-97 (3d Cir. 2011); *United States v. Quinzon*, 643 F.3d 1266, 1270-271 (9th Cir. 2011).

In: Federal Mandatory Minimum Sentencing ISBN 978-1-62081-988-3
Editors: M. J. Davis and A. M. White

Chapter 2

MANDATORY MINIMUM SENTENCING: FEDERAL AGGRAVATED IDENTITY THEFT*

Charles Doyle

SUMMARY

Aggravated identity theft is punishable by a mandatory minimum sentence of imprisonment for two years or by imprisonment for five years if it relates to a terrorism offense. At least thus far, the government has rarely prosecuted the five-year terrorism form of the offense. The two-year offense occurs when an individual knowingly possesses, uses, or transfers the means of identification of another person, without lawful authority to do so, during and in relation to one of more than 60 predicate federal felony offenses (18 U.S.C. 1028A). Section 1028A has the effect of establishing a mandatory minimum sentence for those predicate felony offenses, when they involve identity theft.

A sentencing court has the discretion not to "stack" or pancake multiple aggravated identity theft counts and, as with other mandatory minimums, may impose a sentence of less than the mandatory minimum at the request of the prosecution based on the defendant's substantial assistance.

More than half of the judges responding to a United States Sentence Commission survey felt the two-year mandatory minimum penalty was

---

* This is an edited, reformatted and augmented version of the Congressional Research Service Publication, CRS Report for Congress R42100, dated November 25, 2011.

generally appropriate. The commission's report on mandatory minimum sentencing statutes is mildly complimentary of the provision.

INTRODUCTION

Aggravated identity theft is punishable by imprisonment for two years, and by imprisonment for not more than five years if the offense involves a federal crime of terrorism.[1] Aggravated identity theft only occurs when the identity theft happens "during and in relation" to one of several other federal crimes. It has the effect of establishing a mandatory minimum for each of those predicate offenses that would not otherwise exist.

More than half of the judges who responded to a United States Sentencing Commission survey felt that the two-year mandatory minimum was a generally appropriate sentence.[2] The Sentencing Commission's report on mandatory minimum penalties makes little if any mention of the five-year terrorism penalty and instead directs its attention to the two-year identity theft mandatory minimum.[3] The commission further confines itself to comparatively complimentary observations rather than recommendations, due to the provision's relatively recent emergence and its somewhat unique characteristics.[4]

ELEMENTS

Section 1028A, parsed to its elements, declares:

- Whoever
- during and in relation to
- any felony enumerated in
  - subsection (c) [predicate offense], [or]
  - section 2332b(g)(5)(B) [predicate terrorist offense]
- knowingly
- transfers, possesses, or uses-without lawful authority
- a means of identification- of another person

shall, in addition to the punishment provided for such [predicate offense or predicate terrorist offense], be sentenced to a term of imprisonment of 2 years [or a term of imprisonment of 5 years in the case of terrorist predicate offense].[5]

Whoever

Section 1028A only punishes aggravated identity theft by individuals. Most federal crimes outlaw misconduct by both individuals and organizations, such as corporations, firms, and other legal entities. The Dictionary Act explains that "[i]n determining the meaning of any Act of Congress, unless the context indicates otherwise ... the words 'person' and 'whoever' include corporations, companies, associations, firms, partnerships, societies, and joint stock companies, as well as individuals."[6] Section 1028A is one of those situations when "the context indicates otherwise."

Entities other than individuals can be fined, but they cannot be imprisoned. Section 1028A punishes violations with a flat term of imprisonment, but no fine. Thus, only individuals may be punished for violating the section. For the same reason, persons other than individuals may not incur criminal liability indirectly as principals under 18 U.S.C. 2.[7] Principals are subject to the same penalties, in this case only imprisonment.[8]

Persons other than individuals may, however, incur criminal liability as conspirators. The federal conspiracy statute, 18 U.S.C. 371, outlaws conspiracy to commit any federal crime, including aggravated identity theft.[9] It makes conspiracy punishable by both a fine and a term imprisonment.[10] Thus, it seems possible for a person other than an individual to incur criminal liability for conspiracy to commit aggravated identity theft.

During and in Relation to

The phrase "during and in relation to" describes the connection, necessary for a violation under the section, between the predicate offense and the other identity theft elements. The phrase also appears in the mandatory minimums of 18 U.S.C. 924(c) that apply when a firearm is used "during and in relation to" certain crimes of violence or drug trafficking.[11]

There, the Supreme Court has said the "in relation to" portion of the phrase requires that the firearm "must facilitate or have the potential of facilitating" the predicate offense.[12] This suggests that the "phrase 'in relation to' in §1028A ... means that the 'in relation to' element is met if the identity theft 'facilitates or has the potential of facilitating' that predicate felony."[13] Whether the identity theft occurs "during" the predicate offense depends on the duration of the predicate offense.[14]

Subsection (c) Felony Predicates

Section 1028A recognizes two classes of predicate offenses—one of which involves terrorist offenses and carries a five-year term of imprisonment; the other of which does not and carries a two-year term. Proof of the commission of one of the qualifying predicate offenses is an element of aggravated identity theft.[15] The defendant, however, need not otherwise be charged or convicted of the predicate offense.[16] Moreover, the Constitution's double jeopardy clause, which prohibits multiple punishments for the same offense, bars prosecution for both aggravated identity theft and the parallel identity theft provision.[17] Attached is the list of more than 60 federal theft, fraud, immigration, and related felonies for which the two-year mandatory minimum sentencing provision provides a sentencing floor when identity theft is involved.

Federal Crimes of Terrorism Predicates

The terrorist predicate offenses are the federal crimes of terrorism, listed in 18 U.S.C. 2332b(g)(5)(B), regardless of whether the predicate offense was committed for a terrorist purpose.[18] A list of the close to 50 terrorist predicate offenses also appears below as an attachment. The five-year aggravated identity theft offense seems to have been infrequently prosecuted thus far.[19]

Knowingly

The Supreme Court in *Flores-Figueroa* made clear that the knowledge element colors each of the other elements.[20] The government must prove that the defendant was aware that he transferred, possessed, or used something.[21] It must prove that the defendant was aware that he was doing so without lawful authority.[22] Finally, it must prove that the defendant was aware that the something he unlawfully possessed, transferred, or used was that of another person.[23]

Transfers, Possesses, or Uses

What constitutes a proscribed transfer, possession, or use appears to have been a matter of dispute only rarely, perhaps because of the limitations posed by the other elements. For example, the requirement that possession be knowing and in relation to a predicate offense cabins the otherwise natural scope of the term "possession."

Without Lawful Authority

The "lawful authority" element addresses whether the law permits the defendant to use the identification of another, not whether the defendant has the permission of another to borrow the means of identification. Thus, "the use of another person's social security number to commit a qualifying felony, even with that person's permission, serve[s] as use 'without lawful authority' in violation of §1028A."[24] Moreover, a defendant may be guilty of using the means of identity of another without lawful authority for certain purposes, even though he has lawful authority to use the identification for other purposes.[25]

A Means of Identification

The term "means of identification" in the aggravated identify theft provision draws its meaning from the definition of that term in the generic identity theft provision, 18 U.S.C. 1028.[26] "The 'overriding requirement' of [that] definition is that the means of identification 'must be sufficient to identify a specific individual.'"[27] One court has suggested that use of no more than the name of another would be insufficient,[28] but others have indicated that forging the signature of another constitutes use of the means of identification of another without lawful authority.[29]

Of Another Person

The statute does not extend to the use of a "fake id" that is unidentified with any other person.[30] On the other hand, the "other person" element reaches both the living and dead.[31] Moreover, although only an individual may engage in aggravated identity theft, the victim of such a theft might well include persons who are legal entities rather than individuals.

SENTENCING

Aggravated identity theft sentencing is distinctive in a number of ways. First, violations carry a flat mandatory two-year sentence of imprisonment or a flat mandatory five years for terrorism related offenses.[32] Most federal criminal statutes provide a maximum term of imprisonment ("shall be imprisoned for not more than …").[33] If they require a mandatory minimum sentence, it is usually well below the maximum ("shall be imprisoned not less than …") or the maximum is unstated.[34]

Second, it explicitly states that the sentence imposed for the predicate offenses may not be reduced to account for the mandatory minimum.[35] Third, it explicitly states that as a general rule the two- or five-year sentence may not be served concurrently with any sentence imposed for the predicate offense or another.[36] Finally, it establishes an exception to the general rule under which multiple mandatory minimum sentences under the section may be served concurrently at the discretion of the court when consistent with the Sentencing Guidelines.[37]

The Sentencing Guidelines suggest that in exercising its discretion as to whether to impose consecutive or concurrent sentences for multiple aggravated identity theft violations, a court should consider the statutory sentencing factors mentioned in 18 U.S.C. 3553(a)(2), as well as the nature and seriousness of the offense and the extent to which predicate offenses are related.[38] If the purposes of subsection 3553(a)(2) are better served by imposing consecutive sentences, the court may do so even if the predicate offenses are "grouped" (i.e. are closely related).[39]

As in the case of other mandatory minimum sentencing statutes, a court may sentence a defendant convicted of aggravated identity theft to a term of less than two years pursuant to subsection 3553(e).[40] The prosecution must seek the exception, which is only available on the basis of the defendant's substantial assistance in the investigation or prosecution of a federal crime.[41]

SENTENCING COMMISSION REPORT

The Sentencing Commission's mandatory minimum sentencing report addresses only the two-year mandatory minimum sentencing provisions of 18 U.S.C. 1028A(a)(1).[42] The report's chapter on the two-year subsection offers a statistical view of the aggravated identity theft sentencing under the subsection in FY2010.[43] It notes, among other things, that in that year, 797 of the 1,870 identity theft cases involved aggravated identity theft.[44] The cases were "primarily concentrated in three circuits": the Eleventh (23.8%), the Ninth (16.1%), and the Fourth (14.4%); with "a disproportionately large number of cases in three districts": the Southern District of Florida (103 cases), the Eastern District of Pennsylvania (37 cases), and the Eastern District of Virginia (30 cases).[45] Fifty-five of the 797 offenders received sentences of less than two years by virtue of the substantial assistance they provided prosecutors.[46]

The report's assessment of sentencing under the provision is guardedly laudatory: "The problems associated with certain mandatory minimum penalties are not observed, or are not as pronounced, in identity theft offenses. The Commission believes this is due, in part, to 18 U.S.C. §1028A requiring a relatively short mandatory penalty and not requiring stacking of penalties for multiple counts. The statute is relatively new and is used in only a handful of districts, however, so specific findings are difficult to make at this time."[47]

ATTACHMENTS

Two-Year Predicate Offenses

18 U.S.C. 641 (relating to theft of public money, property, or rewards),

18 U.S.C. 656 (relating to theft, embezzlement, or misapplication by bank officer or employee),

18 U.S.C. 664 (relating to theft from employee benefit plans),

18 U.S.C. 911 (relating to false personation of citizenship),

18 U.S.C. 922(a)(6) (relating to false statements in connection with the acquisition of a firearm),

18 U.S.C. ch. 47 (any provision contained in this chapter (relating to fraud and false statements), other than this section (section 1028A) or section 1028(a)(7):

18 U.S.C. 1001 (relating to false statements or entries generally),
18 U.S.C. 1002 (relating to possession of false papers to defraud United States),
18 U.S.C. 1003 (relating to demands against the United States involving $1,000 or more),
18 U.S.C. 1004 (relating to certification of checks),
18 U.S.C. 1005 (relating to bank entries, reports and transactions),
18 U.S.C. 1006 (relating to Federal credit institution entries, reports and transactions),
18 U.S.C. 1007 (relating to Federal Deposit Insurance Corporation transactions),
18 U.S.C. 1010 (relating to Department of Housing and Urban Development and Federal Housing Administration transactions),
18 U.S.C. 1011 (relating to Federal land bank mortgage transactions),
18 U.S.C. 1014 (relating to loan and credit applications generally; renewals and discounts; crop insurance),
18 U.S.C. 1015 (relating to naturalization, citizenship or alien registry),
18 U.S.C. 1016 (relating to acknowledgment of appearance or oath),
18 U.S.C. 1017 (relating to government seals wrongfully used and instruments wrongfully sealed),
18 U.S.C. 1019 (relating to certificates by consular officers),
18 U.S.C. 1020 (relating to highway projects),
18 U.S.C. 1021 (relating to title records),
18 U.S.C. 1022 (relating to delivery of certificate, voucher, receipt for military or naval property),
18 U.S.C. 1023 (relating to insufficient delivery of money or property for military or naval service),
18 U.S.C. 1024 (relating to purchase or receipt of military, naval, or veteran's facilities property),
18 U.S.C. 1025 (relating to false pretenses on high seas and other waters involving $1,000 or more),
18 U.S.C. 1027 (relating to false statements and concealment of facts in relation to documents required by the Employee Retirement Income Security Act of 1974),

18 U.S.C. 1028 (relating to felony violations involving fraud and related activity in connection with identification documents and information),
18 U.S.C. 1029 (relating to fraud and related activity in connection with access devices),
18 U.S.C. 1030 (relating to felony violations involving fraud and related activity in connection with computers,
18 U.S.C. 1031 (relating to major fraud against the United States),
18 U.S.C. 1032 (relating to concealment of assets from conservator, receiver, or liquidating agent of financial institution),
18 U.S.C. 1033 (relating to crimes by or affecting persons engaged in the business of insurance whose activities affect interstate commerce),
18 U.S.C. 1035 (relating to false statements relating to health care matters),
18 U.S.C. 1036 (relating to entry by false pretenses to any real property, vessel, or aircraft of the United States or secure area of any airport or seaport),
18 U.S.C. 1036 (relating to fraud and related activity in connection with electronic mail),
18 U.S.C. 1038 (relating to false information and hoaxes),
18 U.S.C. 1039 (relating to fraud and related activity in connection with obtaining confidential phone records information of a covered entity),
18 U.S.C. 1040 (relating to fraud in connection with major disaster or emergency benefits),

18 U.S.C. ch. 63 (any provision contained in chapter 63 (relating to mail, bank, and wire fraud);

18 U.S.C. 1341 (relating to mail fraud),
18 U.S.C. 1342 (relating to fraudulent use of false name or address for postal purposes),
18 U.S.C. 1343 (relating to wire fraud),
18 U.S.C. 1344 (relating to bank fraud),
18 U.S.C. 1347 (relating to health care fraud),
18 U.S.C. 1348 (relating to securities fraud),
18 U.S.C. 1349 (relating to attempts or conspiracies to violate the provisions of chapter 63),
18 U.S.C. 1350 (relating to certification of corporate financial reports),
18 U.S.C. 1351 (relating to fraud in foreign labor contracting),

18 U.S.C. ch. 69 (any provision contained in chapter 69 (relating to nationality and citizenship);

18 U.S.C. 1421 (relating to accounts of court officers),
18 U.S.C. 1422 (relating to fees in naturalization proceedings),
18 U.S.C. 1423 (relating to misuse of evidence of citizenship or naturalization),
18 U.S.C. 1424 (relating to misuse of papers in naturalization proceedings),
18 U.S.C. 1425 (relating to procurement of citizenship or naturalization unlawfully),
18 U.S.C. 1426 (relating to reproduction of naturalization or citizenship papers),
18 U.S.C. 1427 (relating to sale of naturalization or citizenship papers),
18 U.S.C. 1428 (relating to surrender of canceled naturalization certificate),
18 U.S.C. 1429 (relating to neglect or refusal to answer naturalization-related subpoena)

18 U.S.C. ch. 75 (any provision contained in chapter 75 (relating to passports and visas);

18 U.S.C. 1541 (relating to issuance without authority),
18 U.S.C. 1542 (relating to false statement in application and use of passport),
18 U.S.C. 1543 (relating to forgery or false use of passport),
18 U.S.C. 1544 (relating to misuse of passport),
18 U.S.C. 1545 (relating to safe conduct violation),
18 U.S.C. 1546 (relating to fraud and misuse of visas, permits, and other documents),

15 U.S.C. 6823 (section 523 of the Gramm-Leach-Bliley Act (relating to obtaining customer information by false pretenses)),

8 U.S.C. 1253 (section 243 of the Immigration and Nationality Act (relating to willfully failing to leave the United States after deportation)),

8 U.S.C. 1306 (section 266 of the Immigration and Nationality Act (relating to creating a counterfeit alien registration card)),

8 U.S.C. ch.12 (any provision contained in chapter 8 of title II of the Immigration and Nationality Act (8 U.S.C. 1321 et seq.) (relating to various immigration offenses);

8 U.S.C. 1321 (relating to prevention of unauthorized landing of aliens),
8 U.S.C. 1324c(e) (relating to document fraud),
8 U.S.C. 1325 (relating to marriage fraud),
8 U.S.C. 1326 (relating to reentry of removed aliens),
8 U.S.C. 1327 (relating to aid or assisting certain aliens to enter),
8 U.S.C. 1328 (relating to importation of alien for immoral purpose)

42 U.S.C. 408 (section 208 of the Social Security Act (relating to penalties for miscellaneous misconduct)),

42 U.S.C. 1011 (section 811 of the Social Security Act (relating to fraud)),

42 U.S.C. 1307(b) (section 1107(b) of the Social Security Act (relating to false statements)),

42 U.S.C. 1320a-7b(a) (section 1128B(a) of the Social Security Act (relating to fraud),

42 U.S.C. 1383a (section 1632 of the Social Security Act (relating to fraud)).

Terrorist Predicate Offenses

18 U.S.C. 32 (relating to destruction of aircraft or aircraft facilities),

18 U.S.C. 37 (relating to violence at international airports),

18 U.S.C. 81 (relating to arson within special maritime and territorial jurisdiction),

18 U.S.C. 175 or 175b (relating to biological weapons),

18 U.S.C. 175c (relating to variola virus),

18 U.S.C. 229 (relating to chemical weapons),

18 U.S.C. 351 (a), (b), (c), (d) (relating to congressional, cabinet, and Supreme Court killing, kidnaping, or attempts or conspiracies to kill or kidnap),

18 U.S.C. 831 (relating to nuclear materials),

18 U.S.C. 832 (relating to participation in nuclear and weapons of mass destruction threats to the U.S.)

18 U.S.C. 842(m) or (n) (relating to plastic explosives),

18 U.S.C. 844(f)(2) or (3) (relating to arson and bombing of Federal property risking or causing death),

18 U.S.C. 844(i) (relating to arson and bombing of property used in interstate commerce),

18 U.S.C. 930(c) (relating to killing or attempted killing during an attack on a Federal facility with a dangerous weapon),

18 U.S.C. 956(a)(1) (relating to conspiracy to murder, kidnap, or maim persons abroad),

18 U.S.C. 1030(a)(1) (relating to protection of computers),

18 U.S.C. 1030(a)(5)(A) resulting in damage as defined in 1030(c)(4)(A)(i)(II) through (VI) (relating to protection of computers),

18 U.S.C. 1114 (relating to killing or attempted killing of officers and employees of the United States),

18 U.S.C. 1116 (relating to murder or manslaughter of foreign officials, official guests, or internationally protected persons),

18 U.S.C. 1203 (relating to hostage taking),

18 U.S.C. 1361 (relating to government property or contracts),

18 U.S.C. 1362 (relating to destruction of communication lines, stations, or systems),

18 U.S.C. 1363 (relating to injury to buildings or property within special maritime and territorial jurisdiction of the United States),

18 U.S.C. 1366(a) (relating to destruction of an energy facility),

18 U.S.C. 1751(a), (b), (c), or (d) (relating to Presidential and Presidential staff killing, kidnaping, or attempts or conspiracies to kill or kidnap),

18 U.S.C. 1992 (relating to terrorist attacks and other acts of violence against mass transit)

18 U.S.C. 2155 (relating to destruction of national defense materials, premises, or utilities),

18 U.S.C. 2156 (relating to national defense material, premises, or utilities),

18 U.S.C. 2280 (relating to violence against maritime navigation),

18 U.S.C. 2281 (relating to violence against maritime fixed platforms),

18 U.S.C. 2332 (relating to certain homicides and other violence against U.S. nationals occurring outside of the U.S.),

18 U.S.C. 2332a (relating to use of weapons of mass destruction),

18 U.S.C. 2332b (relating to acts of terrorism transcending national boundaries),

18 U.S.C. 2332f (relating to bombing of public places and facilities),

18 U.S.C. 2332g (relating to missile systems designed to destroy aircraft),
18 U.S.C. 2332h (relating to radiological dispersal devices),
18 U.S.C. 2339 (relating to harboring terrorists),
18 U.S.C. 2339A (relating to providing material support to terrorists),
18 U.S.C. 2339B (relating to providing material support to terrorist organizations),
18 U.S.C. 2339C (relating to financing of terrorism),
18 U.S.C. 2339D (relating to military-type training from a foreign terrorist organization),
18 U.S.C. 2340A (relating to torture),
21 U.S.C. 960a (section 1010A of the Controlled Substances Import and Export Act) (relating to narco-terrorism),
42 U.S.C. 2122 (section 92 of the Atomic Energy Act of 1954)(relating to prohibitions governing atomic weapons)
42 U.S.C. 2284 (section 236 of the Atomic Energy Act of 1954 (relating to sabotage of nuclear facilities or fuel)
49 U.S.C. 46502 (relating to aircraft piracy),
49 U.S.C. 46504 (second sentence)(relating to assault on a flight crew with a dangerous weapon),
49 U.S.C. 46505(b)(3) or (c) (relating to explosive or incendiary devices, or endangerment of human life by means of weapons, on aircraft),
49 U.S.C. 46506 (if homicide or attempted homicide is involved)(relating to application of certain criminal laws to acts on aircraft),
49 U.S.C. 60123(b) (relating to destruction of interstate gas or hazardous liquid pipeline facility).

End Notes

[1] 18 U.S.C. 1028A(a)(2), (a)(1).

[2] United States Sentencing Commission, *Results of Survey of United States District Judges, January 2010 through March 2010, Question 1* (June 2010), available at More than a quarter of those responding thought the penalty was too high, *id.*, available at http://www.ussc.gov/Research/Research_Projects/Surveys/20100608_Judge_Survey.pdf.

[3] United States Sentencing Commission, *Mandatory Minimum Penalties in the Federal Criminal Justice System (2011 Report)*, 325-44 (Oct. 2011), available at http://www.ussc.gov.

[4] *Id.* at 366-67.

[5] *United States v. Barrington*, 648 F.3d 1178, 1192 (11th Cir. 2011)("To prove a violation of 18 U.S.C. §1028A, the evidence must establish that the defendant: (1) knowingly transferred, possessed, or used; (2) the means of identification of another person; (3) without lawful authority; (4) during and in relation to a felony enumerated in §1028A(c)"); see also, *United States v. Abdelshafi*, 592 F.3d 602, 607 (4th Cir. 2010).

[6] 1 U.S.C.1.

[7] "(a) Whoever commits an offense against the United States or aids, abets, counsels, commands, induces or procures its commission, is punishable as a principal. (b) Whoever willfully causes an act to be done which if directly performed by him or another would be an offense against the United States, is punishable as a principal," 18 U.S.C. 2.

[8] *Id.*

[9] Examples of cases affirming the convictions of individuals charged with conspiracy to commit aggravated identity theft include, *United States v. Blechman*, 657 F.3d 1052, 1054 (10th Cir. 2011), and *United States v. Jenkins-Watts*, 574 F.3d 950, 955 (8th Cir. 2009).

[10] 18 U.S.C. 371 (emphasis added)("If two or more persons conspire either to commit any offense against the United States, or to defraud the United States, or any agency thereof in any manner or for any purpose, and one or more of such persons do any act to effect the object of the conspiracy, *each shall be fined under this title* or imprisoned not more than five years, or both ... ").

[11] 18 U.S.C. 924(c)(1)(A).

[12] *Smith v. United States*, 508 U.S. 223, 239 (1993).

[13] *United States v. Mobley*, 618 F.3d 539, 548-50 (6th Cir. 2010).

[14] See e.g., *United States v. Rodriguez-Moreno*, 526 U.S. 275 (1999)("Section 924(c)(1) criminalized a defendant's use of a firearm 'during and in relation to' a crime of violence; in doing so, Congress proscribed both the use of the firearm and the commission of acts that constitute a violent crime. It does not matter that respondent used the .357 magnum revolver, as the Government concedes, only in Maryland because he did so 'during and in relation to' a kidnaping that was begun in Texas and continued in New York, New Jersey, and Maryland")

[15] *United States v. Curtis*, 635 F.3d 704, 718 n.49 (5th Cir. 2011), citing *Flores-Figueroa v. United States*, 556 U.S. 646 (2009); see also, *United Sates v. Magassouba*, 619 F.3d 202, 205 (2d Cir. 2010); *United States v. Jenkins-Watts*, 574 F.3d 950, 969 (8th Cir. 2009).

[16] *United States v. Jenkins-Watts*, 574 F.3d at 970.

[17] *United States v. Bonilla*, 579 F.3d 1233, 1242-243 (11th Cir. 2009)("[A]ny conduct that would constitute a crime under §1028A(a)(1) would also be a crime covered by the provisions of §1028(a)(7). This is a clear example of one act violating two distinct statutory provisions and therefore violating the protection against double jeopardy").

[18] Subsection 2332b(g)(5) defines "federal crimes of terrorism" as any of the crimes listed in clause 2332b(g)(5)(B), consists of a list of federal crimes, when committed under the circumstances described in clause 2332b(g)(5)(A), that is, when "calculated to influence or affect the conduct of government by intimidation or coercion, or to retaliate against government conduct." Subsection 1028A(a)(2) refers only to the list of offenses in clause (B), and therefore appears to have been intended to dispense with the requirements of clause (A).

[19] As of this date, none of the reported aggravated identity theft cases involved the five-year mandatory minimum sentence that accompanies a terrorism predicate offense, although some courts have mentioned it in their construction of the two-year offenses, e.g., *United States v. Maciel-Alcala*, 612 F.3d 1092, 1098 (9th Cir. 2010); *United Stats v. Godin*, 534 F.3d 51, 59 (1st Cir. 2008).

[20] *Flores-Figueroa v. United States*, 556 U.S 646, 649 (2009)("As a matter of ordinary English grammar, it seems natural to read the statute's word 'knowingly' as applying to all the subsequently listed elements of the crime").

[21] *Id.* (emphasis in the original)("All the parties agree that the provision applies only where the offender knows that he is transferring, possessing, or using *something*").

[22] *Id.* (emphasis in the original)("And the Government reluctantly concedes that the offender likely must know that he is transferring, possessing, or using that *something* without lawful authority").

[23] *Id.* (emphasis in the original)("The question is whether the statute requires the Government to show that the defendant *knew* that the 'means of identification' he or she unlawfully transferred, possessed, or used, in fact, belonged to 'another person.' We conclude that it does"); see also, *United States v. Dvorak*, 617 F.3d 1017, 1025 (8th Cir. 2010).

[24] *United States v. Retana*, 641 F.3d 272, 274-75 (8th Cir. 2011); see also, *United States v. Mobley*, 618 F.3d 539, 547 (6th Cir. 2010).

[25] *United States v. Abdelshafi*, 592 F.3d 602, 608 (4th Cir. 2010)("Abdelshafi came into lawful possess, initially, of Medicaid patients' identifying information and had 'lawful authority' to use that information for proper billing purposes. He did not have 'lawful authority,' however, to use Medicaid patients' identifying information to submit fraudulent billing claims").

[26] *United States v. Barrington*, 648 F.3d 1178, 1193 (11th Cir. 2011). Subsection 18 U.S.C. 1028(d)(7) states that, "the term 'means of identification' means any name or number that may be used, alone or in conjunction with any other information, to identify a specific individual, including any - (A) name, social security number, date of birth, official State or government issued driver's license or identification number, alien registration number, government passport number, employer or taxpayer identification number; (B) unique biometric data, such as fingerprint, voice print, retina or iris image, or other unique physical representation; (C) unique electronic identification number, address, or routing code; or (D) telecommunication identifying information or access device (as defined in section 1029(e))."

[27] *Id.*, quoting *United States v. Mitchell*, 518 F.3d 230, 234 (4th Cir. 2008).

[28] *United States v. Mitchell*, 518 F.3d at 234 ("A name alone, for example, would likely not be sufficiently unique to identify a specific individual because many persons have the same name").

[29] *United States v. Silva*, 554 F.3d 13, 23 n.14 (1st Cir. 2009)("Silva argues a forged prescription containing a forged doctor's name is excluded as a 'means of identification.' ... Silva's contention runs afoul of the plain language of the statute"); see also, *United States v. Blixt*, 548 F.3d 882, 886-88 (9th Cir. 2008).

[30] *Flores-Figueroa v. United States*, 556 U.S. 646, 649 (2009); *United States v. Mobley*, 618 F.3d 539, 547 (6th Cir. 2010); *United States v. Gomez-Castro*, 605 F.3d 1245, 1248 (11th Cir. 2010).

[31] *United States v. LaFuive*, 618 F.3d 613, 617 (7th Cir. 2010); *United States v. Maciel-Alcala*, 612 F.3d 1092, 1096-102 (9th Cir. 2010); *United States v. Kowal*, 527 F.3d 741, 745-47 (8th Cir. 2008); *United States v. Jimenez*, 507 F.3d 13, 18-20 (1st Cir. 2007).

[32] 18 U.S.C. 1028A(a)(1), (a)(2).

[33] E.g., 18 U.S.C. 1341("Whoever, having devised ... any scheme ... to defraud ... places in any post office ... any matter ... shall be ... imprisoned not more than 20 years ... "); 18 U.S.C. 1001(a)(1)(" ... whoever, in any matter within the jurisdiction of the executive ... branch ... of the United States ... (1) falsifies, conceals, or covers up by any trick, scheme, or device any material fact ... shall be ... imprisoned not more than 5 years ... ").

[34] E.g., 21 U.S.C. 841(a)(1)(A)("In the case of a violation of subsection (a) of this section [relating to drug trafficking] involving 1 kilogram or more of ... heroin ... such person shall be sentenced to a term of imprisonment which may not be less than 10 years or more than life ... "); 18 U.S.C. 924(c)(1)(A)(i)(" ... any person who, during and in relation to a crime of violence ... uses or carries a firearm ... shall, in addition to the punishment provided for such crime of violence ... (i) be sentence to a term of not less than 5 years").

[35] 18 U.S.C. 1028A(b) 18 U.S.C. 1028A(b)(3)("[I]n determining any term of imprisonment to be imposed for the felony during which the means of identification was transferred, possessed, or used, a court shall not in any way reduce the term to be imposed for such crime so as to compensate for, or otherwise take into account, any separate term of imprisonment imposed or to be imposed for a violation of this section"). Nevertheless, "a district court, in

sentencing a defendant on a 18 U.S.C. §1028A aggravated identity theft conviction, is not precluded from taking §1028A's mandatory sentence into account in sentencing defendant on *other counts of conviction* charged in the same indictment that are *not predicate felonies* underlying the §1028A conviction," *United States v. Vidal-Reyes*, 562 F.3d 43, 56 (1st Cir. 2009)(emphasis added); *United States v. Wahid*, 614 F.3d 1009, 1014 (9th Cir. 2010). Moreover, sentence imposed for the predicate offense may not be *enhanced* to account for presence of the aggravate identity theft penalty to be imposed, U.S.S.G. §2B1.6, app.n.2; *United States v. Lyons*, 556 F.3d 703, 708 (8th Cir. 2009); *United States v. Sharapka*, 526 F.3d 58, 62 (1st Cir. 2008).

[36] 18 U.S.C. 1028A(b)(2)("[E]xcept as provided in paragraph (4), no term of imprisonment imposed on a person under this section shall run concurrently with any other term of imprisonment imposed on the person under any other provision of law, including any term of imprisonment imposed for the felony during which the means of identification was transferred, possessed, or used").

[37] 18 U.S.C. 1028A(b)(4)("[A] term of imprisonment imposed on a person for a violation of this section may, in the discretion of the court, run concurrently, in whole or in part, only with another term of imprisonment that is imposed by the court at the same time on that person for an additional violation of this section, provided that such discretion shall be exercised in accordance with any applicable guidelines and policy statements issued by the Sentencing Commission pursuant to section 994 of title 28"); see also, *United States v. Vidal-Reyes*, 562 F.3d 43, 50 (1st Cir. 2009)(internal citations omitted)("We note that the only exception to this statutorily mandated rule requiring that all other sentences run consecutively to a sentence under §1028A grants a district court discretion to run additional §1028A sentences imposed at the same time concurrently with each other"); *United States v. Lee*, 545 F.3d 678, 680 (8th Cir. 2008).

[38] U.S.S.G. §5G1.2, app.n. 2.(B)("In determining whether multiple counts of 18 U.S.C. § 1028A should run concurrently with, or consecutively to, each other, the court should consider the following non-exhaustive list of factors: (i) The nature and seriousness of the underlying offenses. For example, the court should consider the appropriateness of imposing consecutive, or partially consecutive, terms of imprisonment for multiple counts of 18 U.S.C. § 1028A in a case in which an underlying offense for one of the 18 U.S.C. § 1028A offenses is a crime of violence or an offense enumerated in 18 U.S.C. § 2332b(g)(5)(B). (ii) Whether the underlying offenses are groupable under §3D1.2 (Groups of Closely Related Counts). Generally, multiple counts of 18 U.S.C. § 1028A should run concurrently with one another in cases in which the underlying offenses are groupable under §3D1.2. (iii) Whether the purposes of sentencing set forth in 18 U.S.C. § 3553(a)(2) are better achieved by imposing a concurrent or a consecutive sentence for multiple counts of 18 U.S.C. § 1028A"); see also, U.S.S.G. §2B1.6, app.n. 1.(B).

[39] *United States v. Collins*, 640 F.3d 265, 269-70 (7th Cir. 2011), citing in accord *United States v. Kreitinger*, 576 F.3d 500, 504 (8th Cir. 2009). Subsection 3553(a)(2) states: "(a) The court shall impose a sentence sufficient, but not greater than necessary, to comply with the purposes set forth in paragraph (2) of this subsection. The court, in determining the particular sentence to be imposed, shall consider ... (2) the need for the sentence imposed - (A) to reflect the seriousness of the offense, to promote respect for the law, and to provide just punishment for the offense; (B) to afford adequate deterrence to criminal conduct; (C) to protect the public from further crimes of the defendant; and (D) to provide the defendant with needed educational or vocational training, medical care, or other correctional treatment in the most effective manner".

[40] E.g., *United States v. Barrington*, 648 F.3d 1178, 1183-184 (11th Cir. 2011); *United States v. Moore*, 581 F.3d 681, 683 (8th Cir. 2009).

[41] 18 U.S.C. 3553(e)("Upon motion of the Government, the court shall have the authority to impose a sentence below a level established by statute as a minimum sentence so as to reflect a defendant's substantial assistance in the investigation or prosecution of another

person who has committed an offense. Such sentence shall be imposed in accordance with the guidelines and policy statements issued by the Sentencing Commission pursuant to section 994 of title 28, United States Code"); the Sentencing Guidelines carry the provision forward along with factors for determining the extent of the appropriate reduction below the minimum, U.S.S.G. §5K1.1.

[42] *2011 Report*, 325-44, 366-69. It says nothing of the five-terrorism provisions of 18 U.S.C. 1028A(a)(2).

[43] *Id.* at 325-44.

[44] *Id.* at 329.

[45] *Id.* at 333-34.

[46] *Id.* at 337.

[47] *Id.* at 369.

INDEX

T

U

V

W